HOOKED RUGS

Other books by William C. Ketchum, Jr.

A TREASURY OF AMERICAN BOTTLES
AMERICAN BASKETRY AND WOODENWARE, A COLLECTOR'S GUIDE
THE POTTERY AND PORCELAIN COLLECTOR'S HANDBOOK
EARLY POTTERS AND POTTERIES OF NEW YORK STATE

HOOKED RUGS

A HISTORICAL AND COLLECTOR'S GUIDE
HOW TO MAKE YOUR OWN

WILLIAM C. KETCHUM, JR.

Introduction
BRUCE JOHNSON
Director, Museum of American Folk Art

Photographs
JOHN GARETTI

Drawings
GARY TONG

Ruggery Section
RICHARD FLYNN

HARCOURT BRACE JOVANOVICH

NEW YORK AND LONDON

DESIGN BY ULRICH RUCHTI

Printed in the United States of America

First edition

B C D E

Library of Congress Cataloging in Publication Data

Ketchum, William C.   1931-
    Hooked rugs: a historical and collector's guide.

    Bibliography: p.
    Includes index.
    1. Rugs, Hooked. I. Title.
TT850.K43   746.7′4   76-13880
ISBN: 0-15-142168-4

IN MEMORY OF
BRUCE JOHNSON

Special thanks to the project editor,
Constance Schrader, who invited me to a lunch
that resulted in this book;
to my copyeditor; and all the production staff
and designers who made this book possible.

CONTENTS

INTRODUCTION

On September 19, 1974 the doors of the Museum of American Folk Art opened a new exhibition and crowds of people poured in as never before. Why? To see HOOKED RUGS IN THE FOLK ART TRADITION. This was the first museum exhibition devoted solely to hooked rugs. The show was so popular that it was extended two months and was then sent on tour to Boston.

Folk art goes beyond the call of duty—it is necessity made beautiful: Floors had to be covered and worn out cloth was too precious to be discarded. The result is a hooked rug. What is amazing is that these anonymous artists had such an innate sense of design, a sense of design that was years ahead of everyone else. With a twentieth-century sophistication, we can now fully appreciate their simple, bold compositions.

By taking rugs from the floor and hanging them on the wall, the Museum showed how beautiful these rugs can be—impressionism and abstract expressionism in rag and burlap—the folk artist scooping the academic artists by fifty to one hundred years, turning rags to riches.

Rug hookers, because of the rigid limitations of the medium, had to compose their pieces in a hard-edged style; they had to learn to use dots of color to create an image or geometric and abstract configurations. These techniques do not emerge and develop in the mainstream of art until the 1900s.

Hooked rugs are folk art and folk art's major strength is its honesty. It conveys the spirit and feelings of the creator. Perspective and proportion are not important. A horse is bigger than a house because to the artist the horse is more important than the house. What is important is that you, as the observer, see what the artist felt.

Recognizing that these rugs are works of art, we must look at them with new eyes. Pick them up and protect and cherish them before they are destroyed. Care for them as we would a painting or a sculpture. Also remember that this art form is not dead. As a matter of fact, it is very simple to do. There is no mixing of oils, kneading and turning of messy clay with kilns and glazes, nor is there the chiseling of wood. You just need lots of rags, a hook, and some burlap. You do not have to be a nineteenth-century pioneer woman. In America "folk" means everyone, it means fun, it means you.

HOOKED RUGS is a useful and valuable multi-purpose book for the scholar, the collector, and the would-be, or soon to be, artist. I admire Bill Ketchum's frank advice to buyers of hooked rugs, and I advise all buyers of antiquities to learn from Mr. Ketchum's experience.

For those who prefer to make their own—read Richard Flynn's section carefully and do not hesitate to rip up your old clothes and begin hooking—you may find your work on our Museum walls some day soon.

BRUCE JOHNSON
Museum of American Folk Art

PART I
A HISTORICAL AND COLLECTOR'S GUIDE

THE MAKING OF A HOOKED RUG

The widespread interest in rug hooking, both in the nineteenth century and at present, did not develop by accident. It was directly related to the relative simplicity of the craft and to the practicality, charm, and attractiveness of the finished product. The making of hooked floor coverings is a most pleasant and satisfying hobby: it requires little formal training and quite inexpensive tools and materials, and it offers endless opportunities for creative expression. As a Tennessee farmwife once wrote to the *Rural New Yorker*:

I enjoy making my own designs. I never knew how to sing or paint or draw; no way to express myself, only by hoeing, washing, ironing, patching, etc., and while I never hope to accomplish anything extraordinary, I do love to plan out and execute these rugs that are a bit of myself, a blind groping after something beautiful.

So often practitioners of the fine and applied arts discover that the pleasure of striving to create something beautiful is hindered by the complexity of the medium in which they are working. Rug making, an enjoyable and uncomplicated craft, presents no such obstacle.

Techniques

Although dates of origin have not been firmly established, the so-called "yarn-sewn" textiles apparently antedate hooked examples. Quite a few authenticated eighteenth-century specimens of yarn-sewn textiles have come down to us, but no hooked textiles of comparable age. The techniques used in these allied arts, however, are sufficiently similar to make one suspect that they have coexisted for a long time.

The yarn-sewn rug is constructed by working yarn through a fabric base in a continuous running stitch. This stitch is drawn up tight on the reverse, or bottom, of the textile while leaving loose-standing loops on the surface. The loops are placed sufficiently close together to support each other. By varying stitches and colors, elaborate compositions can be created. In most cases, the loop tops are clipped off to leave a soft pile surface remarkably similar to that found in a hooked rug.

Although yarn-sewn textiles were popular in Canada and along the North Atlantic coast during the eighteenth century, the craft seems to have lost favor soon after 1800. In the examples that have survived, wool yarn and linen backing were used. Sometimes tow (coarse woven flax or hemp) was also used for backing, except in the case of "Bedd Ruggs," as some of the old blankets or comforters were called. For these, wool backings were used. All goods were homespun and colored with natural dyes. Although jute burlap is by far the most commonly used base material in hooked rugs, there are, to my knowledge, no existing yarn-sewn specimens with burlap backing.

Floral: Hooked, clipped
rag on burlap, 34" x 53".
Red, tan, and brown
floral on yellow ground.
Late nineteenth century.
Courtesy Dalmar Tift
and Ilon Spect.

Despite the fact that the resulting textile is quite similar in appearance to that achieved by yarn sewing, hooked rugs differ from yarn-sewn rugs in several ways. Most basic is the method of construction. In the yarn textile, a continuous piece of thick thread is sewn in and out through the backing with a large needle. In rug hooking, on the other hand, lengths of yarn or strips of cut cloth, usually no more than a foot long, are drawn up through the backing by means of a hooked tool especially made for this task. The loops thus formed support one another on the surface, as in a yarn-sewn piece. Meanwhile, the strips are pulled tight against the base on the reverse, thus creating a duplicate of the pattern on the top surface. The closer together the loops are placed, the tighter the pile.

Another difference between yarn-sewn and hooked textiles is in the material used for backing. In a few hooked rugs canvas or homespun linen backings were used. But, because these backings were too tightly woven to permit entry of the hook and accompanying cloth strip, it was necessary for the worker to punch out his design on the material first. Needless to say, this was a time-consuming task. This problem was solved in the mid-nineteenth century by the introduction of burlap, a coarse sacking material with an extremely loose crosshatch weave that easily admitted the hooking tool.

At first, burlap was obtained from discarded meal or produce bags. As a result, some of the early rugs are unusually small or lopsided, an interesting clue to the source of their base material. Shortly after the Civil War, however, it apparently became possible to purchase roll burlap in more suitable sizes, and soon pieces of jute cut to size and stamped with stenciled rug patterns were being commercially produced. The rise of this industry is discussed in the following chapter.

The finished pile on a hooked rug surface may be clipped or unclipped, as in yarn-sewn textiles. Both creators and collectors tend to prefer one or the other surface. W. W. Kent, in his early and interesting text, *The Hooked Rug*, spoke for the natural finish:

As to varieties of texture, which produce different effects according to their surfaces, the unclipped rug, wherein the loops are drawn tightly to a low and even height and so left, is, in the opinion of many critics, the most beautiful and the most durable, as well as the most difficult to make.

Kent maintained that ". . . the best unclipped hooked rugs have the effect of good mosaic, in fact they are mosaics in cloth. . . ."

Clipped rugs, however, have always been popular. Some theorize that the style may have been inspired by old carpets whose surface had been worn down by use. This seems unlikely, though, since the technique was known in ancient times and was also employed on the yarn-sewn Bedd Ruggs, where such heavy wear would be most unlikely. In any case, although the charm of the matted felt-like surface achieved by clipping can hardly be doubted, to clip or not to clip is today purely a matter of individual taste.

Types of Hooked Rugs

Hooked rugs come in a fascinating variety of shapes and sizes, many of which reflect the different uses for which they were intended. The smallest are not properly rugs at all, but rather doilies and seat covers. Circular in shape, they range in size from 8 to 16 inches in diameter. Most specimens are made from factory cotton yarn and commercial patterns, and appear to date from the early twentieth century.

At the other end of the spectrum are room-sized carpets. Perhaps the largest of these ever made was the 18-by-36-foot monster created in 1938 as a floor covering for the Queen of England's bedchamber upon the occasion of her visit to Ottawa, Canada. It took eight women six months to complete. As a general rule, the larger the rug, the more valuable it is likely to be. This is because larger pieces are more difficult to complete, since it is necessary to roll back completed portions as the hooking progresses. This makes the work bulky and awkward to handle. Most room-sized carpets seen in antique shops today are not hand-hooked but factory-made reproductions created during the hooked-rug craze of the 1920's and 1930's. They are readily recognizable from their uniform commercial yarn and pale pastel color schemes. They are definitely not recommended for collectors.

Between the very small and the very large is a whole raft of other shapes and sizes. Most common is the rectangular rug, but round, square, and oval rugs are also frequently seen. In rare cases square pieces may have been intended for table covers, though without a family history this is usually almost impossible to determine.

Less often seen are the semicircular or half-oval rugs that were used in front of doorways and that often bear legends such as WELCOME or COME AGAIN. These are discussed in some detail in a later chapter. Also somewhat uncommon are the long, thin stair and hall runners, some of which are as much as 25 feet long. While most of these are in the plain striped pattern known as "hit or miss," rare floral and pictorial examples are also seen.

Shapes other than those mentioned above are unusual. One may run across an octagonal or hexagonal piece or one whose edge is scalloped or scrolled to conform to the inner rug design. Least common of all, perhaps, is the hearth rug, which is rectangular in shape but bears a three-sided design.

Most hooked textiles are in the 2-by-3- to 3-by-5-foot range with larger and smaller specimens increasing in rarity and value as they change in size. Large and small pictorials are regarded as particularly choice.

Design Influences

So many and so varied are the designs on American hooked rugs that one might write a book about this subject alone. Anyone with more than a superficial knowledge of the decorative arts can have a field day analyzing these patterns. Here is a flat copy of an Aubusson rug, here a transposition of motifs common to Canton, China, and there something that was made by drawing circles around a teacup.

To a limited extent, it is possible to categorize these various influences. The earliest are European. Kent traces the familiar scroll border to the turnings on Tudor furniture. Old china such as Staffordshire and majolica also provided inspiration, as did imported textiles like Paisley shawls and cotton prints. And, of course, English, continental, and Eastern rugs played a major role in shaping the style of their homespun American counterparts. This is discussed in some detail in a subsequent chapter.

Even more clearly recognizable are domestic influences and regional variations. The very earliest hooked rugs of the northeast show the same "wandering" vine decoration that was used in yarn-sewn fabrics. In the Atlantic coastal regions there are nautical rugs bearing devices indistinguishable from those seen on painted sea chests. In Pennsylvania practically identical tulip motifs appear both on dower chests and hooked textiles.

Woven coverlets of the 1820–1840 period and patchwork quilts also were copied by rug makers, and the familiar log cabin design is seen frequently on both quilts and rugs. Kent illustrates a hooked version of the old "Star of Bethlehem" design that is a dead ringer for the quilt. It is quite likely that many such rugs were copied from the quilt patterns that appeared regularly in women's magazines such as *Godey's Ladies' Book*.

And there were still other sources of inspiration. Wallpaper and the painted oilcloth floor coverings so popular before 1830 could have provided ideas. The Spencerian style of handwriting was so widely taught in the last half of the nineteenth century that it too spawned a host of designs. The list, and the fascinating speculation it invites, could go on and on, for the interchange between the various crafts over the course of the last century was widespread. Our interest, however, lies chiefly in what the rug makers did with these designs from other arts.

Materials

As was noted earlier, only a few tools and materials are required to hook a rug. To begin with, one needs either burlap or canvas for backing, and yarn or any kind of fabric, old or new. To this add a hook. Although only a few decades ago a filed nail or large crochet hook might have sufficed, today's hooks are modern mechanical devices. The final item is a frame. Though some people prefer to hook rugs on their laps, the use of a frame is customary.

The limited number of materials used for backing has already been discussed. Let's now take a closer look at exactly how some of the early rugs were made. The first pieces were made primarily of virgin wool spun into a coarse yarn. If there was not enough wool available, the figures were usually done in wool and the ground in rag. Because the bulky homespun could not be tightly hooked, the early rugs were very loosely woven. As a result, they were not particularly durable, which probably explains why so few of them have survived.

In Pennsylvania and New Jersey, tufts of unspun wool were sometimes pulled through the backing. Again, the result was a thick but fragile rug. Woolen worsted material proved to last far longer, and many examples composed wholly or in part of worsted have survived from the late nineteenth and early twentieth centuries. Wool is still popular with modern rug makers. One commercial supplier offers rug wool by the yard in no fewer than 60 colors.

Many other fabrics also ended up in hooked textiles. Almost any old cloth would do. Cotton, particularly in the form of unprinted calico, has always been common, despite the fact that it has serious drawbacks. It is harsh in texture, it fades quickly, and it tends to deteriorate after only a few washings. Much the same may be said of linen, which also was used in the very earliest rugs. Although linen is more durable than cotton, it too lacks the soft texture and deep pile so appealing in a woolen rug.

Materials such as felt, hemp or rope, and burlap were less frequently used. Because most of these materials are extremely coarse and unattractive, they were used only for background, and then only by a worker especially short of fabric. Felt, though soft, probably came from an old horse blanket, and thus bore the aroma of its former use. W. W. Kent once remarked, upon being offered yet another specimen with the telltale odor, that "the love of hooked rugs is not an acquired taste but an acquired smell."

Silk, generally the remnants of a long-treasured wedding dress, is also occasionally seen in hooked rugs. In Kentucky, in the 1930's, silk stockings were often hooked into small items such as seat covers, which were noticeably soft and flexible.

In short, particularly before the advent of commericial material suppliers, a great variety of materials was used in hooked rugs. More than one collector has spent a happy afternoon trying to figure out just what did go into his latest acquisition!

Color

The use of color in old hooked rugs, like the use of materials, reflects both taste and necessity. The earlier rugs differ greatly from those of the late Victorian era, and there are also frequent regional differences.

Most rugs made prior to the Civil War either were colored with dyes derived from natural sources, or they possessed the color of the rags from which they were made. Most specimens of this period tend to be somewhat somber in hue. Red, yellow, green, brown, gray, and black were the most frequently used colors.

This limited palette was partially a matter of personal preference, and partially a reflection of the difficulties involved in home dye making. Preparing dyes was a craft in itself. It required the gathering of roots and herbs, the boiling of the dye with a "mordant" or natural fixitive such as alum to prevent the color from washing out too quickly, and the controlled steeping of the fabric in order to achieve a more or less uniform hue. Given the problems involved, it is not surprising that many rug makers chose to limit themselves to a few shades.

It should be noted, though, that if a dye maker had the skill and the necessary raw materials, a remarkable variety of tints could be obtained from natural sources. The following list quoted from Douglas Leechman's article, "The Magic Dyes of Olden Days" (*American Home*, March, 1930), suggests what was available.

RED: Alder, bedstraw, bloodroot, cedar, cranberry, dogwood, elm, grape, gromwell, hemlock, hooked-crow-foot, lamb's quarters, maple, sorrel, spruce roots, sumac, tamarack.

YELLOW: Alder, barberry, beech, blue beech, crab apple, goldenrod, goldenseal, goldthread, hickory, marsh marigold, oak, poplar, prickly ash, quercitron, sassafras, sumac, sunflower, touch-me-not, willow.

BLACK: Alder, poison ivy, sumac, walnut.

ORANGE: Alder, bittersweet, dodder, sassafras, touch-me-not.

GREEN: Ash, hound's tongue, mint, smartweed, walnut, yellow adder's-tongue.

PURPLE: Blueberry, elderberry, huckleberry.

BROWN: Alder, butternut, oak, walnut.

BLUE: Grape, larkspur, oak, spruce bark, sycamore, toadflax.

If you are intimidated by the thought of locating plants with such exotic names as hooked-crow-foot and quercitron, or of gathering such potent sources as poison ivy and sumac, it is quite likely that your predecessors probably felt the same way. One thing is sure. They much preferred imported coloring agents such as cochineal for red, logwood for black, and indigo for blue, even though imported dyes were often fairly expensive.

With the introduction in the late nineteenth century of modern coal-tar and aniline dyes, home dye making decreased. The ready availability of a wide color spectrum was particularly pleasing to Victorian tastes. Rugs were flooded with color: a dozen different hues might appear in the same piece. Pure white backgrounds and black borders, previously rare, became common, particularly in parlor rugs. Needless to say, there were often violent contrasts in color, and these are seldom pleasing to the sophisticated modern eye. Fortunately the early factory-made dyes were not particularly lasting. As John Ramsey commented in his article, "A Note on the Geography of Hooked Rugs" (*Antiques Magazine*, December, 1930), Victorian ". . . coloring is raw and often glaring, but rarely permanent, so that even the most clamorous notes are in time reduced to a whisper."

Regional differences, though perhaps less obvious than contrasts of period, also exist. Even in the very early rugs there were substantial differences between the subtle tones of the New England textiles and the brighter Acadian floor coverings. Later on, the rugs of Nova Scotia were characterized by minimal use of color—blacks and grays predominated, with dark green highlights and rare spots of red or yellow. Neighboring Maine and New Hampshire, however, employed a much more extensive palette. Farther south, in Pennsylvania, a variety of brilliant hues were thrown together upon a dark background. Very little research has yet been done into these distinctions, but there is no doubt that they exist and that they will provide a fascinating field for future research.

The Rug Maker

What about the people who made the early rugs? Today, as we know, rug makers are mainly hobbyists and as likely to be men or children as women. But in the nineteenth century, if Frost's account (see page 14) can be taken as a general rule, they were primarily women, both farmwives and city dwellers. Though some produced hundreds of rugs, most were lucky to turn out two in a season of part-time work, the art usually being limited to winter, except in Newfoundland where it was always traditional to put rugs into the frame in the spring of the year. Rug making is generally thought of as a solitary pastime. Yet, in the Appalachians during the 1920's and 1930's, it was not unusual to find whole families cooperating in the making of a rug. It is a time-consuming craft (a contemporary rug maker in Machias, Maine, told me that it took her approximately 120 hours of steady work to do an average floral pattern), yet it is seldom a tiring one. The people who for years have maintained the skills of rug making have a steady following, for their craft has spread and is increasing in popularity.

THE ORIGIN AND DEVELOPMENT OF RUG MAKING

Unlike most American antiquities and folk crafts, the hooked rug does not have a long and well-documented history. Pottery can be traced back through known artisans to the mid-eighteenth century; silver, pewter, and glass to an even earlier date. The hooked rug, on the other hand, seems to burst upon us quite suddenly around 1850. Where had the craft been until then?

Unfortunately, the few dated examples that exist are all from the second half of the nineteenth century. Perhaps the early rug hookers were an exceedingly modest lot, though this could hardly be said for craftswomen in general. After all, they had been signing and dating samplers and memorial pictures since the early 1700's. Contemporary references are also rare. The earliest is an announcement in an 1838 program of the Maine Charitable Mechanics' Association of a prize for "the best hooked rug."

Despite the lack of well-documented evidence, however, there seems little doubt that the craft of rug hooking was practiced here as well as in other countries much earlier than the nineteenth century. W. W. Kent and other early enthusiasts spent a good deal of time and effort trying to track down the origin of the craft. They came up with some information and a good deal of speculation. To begin with, someone noted that the "stitching" in a hooked rug (technically, what is involved is not a stitch but rather a pulling up) resembles the chain stitch used in ancient East Indian tambour work. The Indian textile bears little resemblance to a hooked rug, however, and what similarity there is serves rather to support the historical truism that extremely simple techniques may be developed independently at various times and places.

This surmise is borne out by the existence of hooked Egyptian textiles dating to the fifth century A.D., and similar work from the Las Alpuharras district of Spain, to which it was brought by the Moors. The Moors, of course, could quite conceivably have learned the craft while they were in Egypt. But this was all a long time past and does not have much bearing on rugs that were made only a hundred or so years ago.

Scandinavian and European sources are more relevant. Certain Finnish peasant rugs bear distinct resemblances to the hooked rug both in appearance and mode of manufacture. Since the Finns and other seafaring Scandinavians paid frequent visits to the British Isles, researchers looked there for the next link. They felt that they had found it in the hearth mats that were manufactured in Yorkshire and in Scotland during the early nineteenth century. These so-called "brodded" or "pegged" floor coverings were made from woolen yarn ends salvaged from loom waste by cottage weavers. The ends were pulled through a coarse backing to form a rough pile. The technique used was identical to that employed by English and continental seamen in making thrum mats, a procedure described later in this book.

Brodded rug making appears to have been an extensive British cottage industry (these rugs were advertised in 1821 issues of the

Floral: Hooked rag on
burlap, 31" x 47.5".
Elaborate pattern of
leaves and flowers in
wine, tan, and green.
Early twentieth century.
Courtesy Dalmar Tift
and Ilon Spect.

Manchester Guardian), and one may therefore assume with some justification that the skill was thus known to the English and Scottish settlers of Nova Scotia and northern New England. Indeed, the earliest references to the art on this continent are traceable to these localities. Moreover, most of the best free-hand work comes from the same area. The French-speaking pioneers of Acadia would have been familiar with the art either through European influences or through familiarity with sailors' thrum mats.

An important question still remains: How soon after their arrival on these shores did these immigrants begin to make hooked rugs? Some feel that few rugs were made prior to 1825, and that the major period of rug making was after 1850. This may well be true if one defines a hooked rug solely as one that is made by pulling up cloth through the interstices in a backing. Certainly, the introduction into the country during the 1850's of cheap jute burlap from the Indies offered for the first time a widely available and particularly suitable base material for this method.

Rugs were also made with punched linen and canvas bases, however: the art was not dependent upon burlap. Moreover, yarn-sewn rugs, as previously noted, are essentially similar in effect to hooked textiles, and several existing specimens of this type date to the eighteenth century, including some with the specific dates of 1782 and 1799. There were also yarn-sewn table and chest covers. The apparent nonexistence of similar floor coverings may simply reflect the greater wear to which rugs were subjected, and consequently their shorter life span. It may also, of course, indicate that the technique was not used for rugs at that time. A cloth rug takes a good deal of material, old or new, and textiles were for many decades in short supply among average citizens. All available scraps may have gone into quilts and other bed coverings.

It should not be assumed, however, that floor coverings were uncommon in the colonies. Quite the contrary. If one had the money, a great variety of rugs and carpets could be obtained, as may be seen from the following merchant's notice in the August 27, 1798, edition of the *New York Gazette and General Advertiser:*

A. S. Norwood Carpet Store. A. S. Norwood, impressed with a deep sense of gratitude for the many favors he has received in the line of upholsterer, takes this method to inform his friends that he has now opened a carpet store at No. 127 William Street, where he has just received from some of the finest manufactures in Europe an assortment of carpets and carpeting . . . consisting of striped Brussels carpeting for stairs and entries, 1–2 yd., 3–4 and 7–8; Venetian, 7–8 & 4–4; English ingrained, 4–4; Scotch ingrained, do, 4–4 . . . Common Scotch, do, . . . an assortment of hearth rugs.

How helpful it would be to see some of those hearth rugs! Might they not prove to be the brodded rugs of Scotland and northern England that were being offered for sale a quarter century later?

It is clear that floor coverings of many sorts were well known to eighteenth-century inhabitants of North America. The poor, who could not afford imported varieties, must surely have had some substitute. Given the climatic conditions, rugs would have been a necessity rather than a luxury. The bitter winters and chill winds of the northeastern seaboard demanded some sort of covering for the crude, sawn log floors of the settlers' homes. What better protection underfoot than a thick and sturdy hooked rug?

That such textiles were made during the eighteenth century is further indicated by the fact that when the first collectors ventured into the Acadian region of eastern Canada during the early years of this century, the rugs they found were careful copies of Aubusson, Moguette, and Savonnaire carpets, all of which were popular in the eighteenth century. Perhaps the artisans simply copied family heirlooms of a much earlier period. Perhaps, but it would seem more likely that a craftswoman working in the mid-nineteenth century would have favored the machine-made Axminster carpets or Orientals then so much in vogue rather than floor coverings already decades out of style.

Whatever the case may be, it seems likely that we will never really know when rug hooking was introduced to North America. What is clear, though, is that by 1840, at the latest, the craft was widespread throughout the Northeast. It was probably practiced in other areas as well. The Acadian migrants who took the skill to Cape Cod later carried it to Louisiana. Finns took it to New Jersey, the Dutch to New York, and the Swedes to Delaware. Pennsylvania, Virginia, North Carolina, and Tennessee were also producing hooked textiles by the middle of the last century. In western Maryland, Scottish miners, who arrived about 1840, introduced the craft of rug making. Some extremely attractive pieces were made in this area. It was in eastern Canada and New England, however, that the finest work was done.

The earliest rugs in all areas appear to have been florals, though some would argue for geometrics on the ground that they were easier to produce. Since at first there were no standard commercial patterns, each maker would create free-hand designs using whatever decorative elements seemed appropriate to her. This creative process, which is more fully described in later chapters, was probably seldom completely spontaneous. Floor coverings from a given locality tend to resemble each other. John Ramsey, in his article, "A Note on the Geography of Hooked Rugs," described a Scottish community in Lonaconing Township, Maryland, which produced hooked rugs distinctly different from those manufactured in Pennsylvania Dutch communities no more than five miles away. And, in the area of Waldoboro, Maine, a group of women inspired with the formal craftmanship of Acadia turned out many highly elaborate floral rugs, while all around them contemporaries were working in the more sparse New England manner. In each case there was a strong tradition of creative teachers who could develop and "draw off" patterns for their less talented sisters.

Every art form, of course, produces a few leaders and many followers, and it is for the latter that patterns are made. In a more primitive culture, at an earlier time, the most highly skilled practitioners would have influenced others by example and teaching. Rug hooking, however, was, in its maturity, a product of the Industrial Revolution. As the machine began to assert itself in the years following the Civil War, its greedy fingers fell upon the craft. The instrument of this domination was Edward Sands Frost, a young Civil War veteran from Biddeford, Maine. Although there may well have been others who made standard hooked rug patterns at an earlier time, their names have vanished, and it is Frost who is universally credited with the development of the first commercial rug design. His story is a fascinating example of the rise of the industrial middle class, a true-to-life rendition of the Horatio Alger legend, complete with suffering and triumph.

Because of ill health, Frost was mustered out of the Union Army in 1863. As a result of the same condition, he was forced shortly thereafter to abandon his trade of machinist. He then chose to become a tin peddler, and followed this business with modest success for about five years. Then, as is so often the case with businessmen, an idea forced itself upon him. In 1888, long after the event, he told the story to a reporter for the *Biddeford Times:*

It was during the winter of '68 that my wife, after saving quite a quantity of colored rags that I had collected in my business as a tin peddler, decided to work them into a rug. She went to her cousin, the late Mrs. George Twombley, and had her mark out a pattern, which she did with red chalk on a piece of burlap. After my wife had the piece properly adjusted to her quilting frame, she began to hook in the rags with the instrument then used in rug making, which was a hook made of a nail or an old gimlet. After watching her work a while I noticed that she was using a very poor hook, so, being a machinist, I went to work and made the crooked hook which was used so many years afterward in the rug business, and is still in vogue to-day.

While making the hook I would occasionally try it on the rug to see if it was all right as to size, and in this way I got interested in the rug. I had "caught the fever" as they used to say. So every evening I worked on the rug until it was finished, and it was while thus engaged that I first conceived the idea of working up an article that is to-day about as staple as cotton cloth and sells the world over. Every lady that ever made a rug knows that it is very pleasant and bewitching [to] work on a pretty design, but tiresome and hard on plain figure; and so it proved to me. After working four evenings on the rug I told my wife that I thought I could make a better design myself than that we were at work on, so after we finished our rug I got a piece of burlap and taking a pencil, I wrote my first design on paper and then put it on to the cloth and worked the flower and scroll already for the background.

We showed it to our neighbors and they were so well pleased with it that I got orders for some twenty or more patterns like it within three days. So you see I got myself into business right away. I put in my time evenings and stormy days sketching designs, giving only the outlines in black. There was not money enough in it to devote my whole time to the business, and as the orders came in faster than I could fill them I began, Yankee-like, to study some way to do them quicker. Then the first idea of stencilling presented itself to me.

Did I go to Boston to get my stencils made? Oh, no, I went out into my stable where I had some old iron and some old wash boilers I had bought for their copper bottoms, took the old tin off them and made my first stencil out of it. Where did I get the tools? Why I found them in the same place, in my stable among the old iron. I got there some old files, half flat and half round, took them to the tin shop of Cummings & West and forged my tools to cut the stencil with. I made a cutting block out of old lead and zinc.

After fitting myself out with tools I began making small stencils of single flowers, scrolls, leaves, buds, etc., each one on a small plate; then I could with a stencil brush print in ink in plain figures much faster than I could sketch. Thus I had reduced ten hours' labor to two and a half hours. I then had the art down fine enough to allow me to fill all my orders, so I began to print patterns and put them in my peddler's cart and offer them for sale. The news of my invention of stamped rugs spread like magic, and many a time as I drove through the streets of Biddeford and Saco, a lady would appear at the door or window swinging an apron or sun bonnet and shouting at the top of her voice, say "Are you the rug man? Do you carry rugs all marked out?" I at once became known as Frost, the rug man, and many Biddeford citizens still speak of me in that same way.

My rug business increased and I soon found that I could not print fast enough; I also found it difficult to duplicate my patterns, or to make two exactly alike, as many of my customers would call for a pattern just like Mrs. So and So's. Then I began to make a whole design on one plate. At first it seemed impossible, but I was willing to try, so I obtained a sheet of zinc and printed on it and cut out a design. This process I continued to follow till I had some fourteen different designs on hand, ranging from a yard long and a half wide to two yards long and a yard wide. These plates gave only the outline in black and required only one impression to make a complete pattern, yet it was by far the hardest part of the whole affair to make the stencils so as to take a good impression, and I think there is not a stencil workman in this country that would consider it possible to cut so large a plate with such fine figures and take an impression from it. It required a great deal of patience, for I was just thirty days cutting the first one and when I laid it on the table the center of the plate would not touch the table by two and a half inches. As the plate of zinc lay smooth before being cut, I knew it must be the cutting that caused the trouble; I studied into the problem and learned that in cutting, the metal expanded, so I expanded the uncut portion in proportion to that which was cut and the plate then lay smooth. This I did with a hammer, and it took about two days' time.

When the plate was finished I could print with it a pattern in four minutes that had previously required ten hours to sketch by hand. I then thought I had my patterns about perfect, so I began to prepare them for the market. I remember well the first trip I made through Maine and a part of New Hampshire, trying to sell my goods to the dry goods trade. I failed to find a man who dared to invest a dollar in them; in fact, people did not know what they were for, and I had to give up trying for a while and go from house to house. There I found plenty of purchasers, for I found the ladies knew what the patterns were for.

Next I began coloring the patterns by hand, as I had some call for colored goods. The question of how to print them in colors so as to sell them at a profit seemed to be the point on which the success of the whole business hung, and it took me over three months to settle it. I shall never forget the time and place it came to me, for it had become such a study that I could not sleep nights. It was in March, 1870, one morning about two o'clock. I had been thinking how I could print the bright colors in with the dark ones so as to make good clear prints. My mind was so fixed on the problem that I could not sleep, so I turned and twisted and all at once I seemed to hear a voice in my room say: "Print your bright colors first and then the dark ones." That settled it, and I was so excited that I could not close my eyes in sleep the rest of the night and I tell you I was glad when morning came so that I could get to town to buy stock for the plates with which to carry out my idea.

At the end of a week I had one design made and printed in colors. It proved a success. Then I sold my tin peddling business and hired a room in the building on Main Street just above the savings bank where I began in the month of April (1870) to print patterns in colors. I did my own work at first for three months and then I employed one man. In September I had two men in my employ, and in November I opened a salesroom in Boston through Gibbs & Warren. Then it took four men in December and ten men during the rest of the winter. Many of the businessmen here will remember what an excitement my business created, for there were very few men who had any faith in my bonanza. I remember having seen well-known businessmen stand in the street near Shaw's block and point over at my goods that were hung out and laugh at the idea (as they afterward told me) of my making a living out of such an undertaking. Well, I guess they will all admit that I did make a living out of it, as I continued to manufacture rug patterns there, all of my own designs, till the fall of '76, when I was so reduced in health that I sold out my business and left Biddeford.

James A. Strout, to whom Frost sold his concern, continued to be active until 1900. The magnitude of this business and the effect it must have had, particularly on rug making in New England, may be judged by the fact that, when Strout closed his doors, he sold some *four tons* of zinc, tin, iron, and copper stencils to one Henry F. Whiting of Lowell, Massachusetts. Nearly all of these were made either

Floral: Hooked yarn on
burlap, 30" x 51.5".
Christmasy floral in red,
tan, and green on a blue-
gray ground. Twentieth
century. Courtesy Dal-
mar Tift and Ilon Spect.

from Frost's designs or from those commissioned by him. The Frost stencils, incidentally, passed from Whiting's widow to Charlotte Stratton of Montpelier, Vermont, a well-known devotee of the craft.

Frost and Strout were not alone in their endeavor. During the last quarter of the nineteenth century, various competitors entered the field. The Oriental Rug Company of Boston boasted that it would furnish patterns stamped in color on white burlap which were ". . . rich and handsome in design, many of them similar to those exhibited at the Great Centennial in the Oriental and Turkish department." The company's literature assured any lady of "ordinary skill and taste" that with these designs she could readily hook a floor covering ". . . fit to grace the parlor of a prince."

Other rug-pattern manufacturers are known primarily by their catalogs, copies of which have been preserved. There is a small pattern book in black and white dating from 1892, which was issued by John L. Garrett of New Glasgow, Nova Scotia. For each composition it specifies a design number, size, colors, and amount and cost of material required, including burlap pattern, wool, cotton, frame, and hooking tool. Garrett, who was active for many years, transferred his business in the twentieth century to Malden, Massachusetts. Another Garrett, John E., possibly a son, issued a small folder of 16 rug designs from his base of operations in Burlington, Vermont. In the Midwest, E. Ross & Company of Toledo, Ohio, was the major supplier. In 1891 they published a brochure containing 56 crudely colored prints of rug patterns, primarily florals. The names H. Pond and Ayers also appear in references as suppliers of commercial compositions, and one can be sure that there were many other such manufacturers, whose contributions are now forgotten.

The availability of prepared designs undoubtedly had a very great influence upon American rug hooking. Women who lacked the creative skill to transpose designs from decorative objects such as china or quilts, and who did not have a neighbor who could "draw off" a pattern for them, were now able to achieve most satisfactory results. And, regardless of how some later collectors might feel about them, the original stencils were often held in high artistic repute by the communities in which they circulated. One of Frost's designs received an award at the Boston Mechanics' Fair of 1878, and the fact that a rug might be based on a commercial pattern was never considered a disqualifying factor at the various county fairs where rug-hooking competitions were held.

There is, on the other hand, no doubt that the overall quality of rug design declined throughout the 1880's and 1890's. This was certainly due in part to the stultifying effect of ready-made patterns on individual creativity, but it is also traceable to the introduction during this period of relatively inexpensive, mass-produced carpeting. Moreover, as is well known, after the Industrial Revolution, handcrafts in general declined in popularity.

During the period of decline, however, the practice of rug making did not vanish. It lingered on until revived in the late Victorian era by a developing middle-class interest in the folk arts. This interest differed substantially from that previously enjoyed by the craft, and it had a profound effect upon it. Throughout the 1800's, rug making was a household necessity. The artisans were generally farmwives and fisherwomen who made rugs because they could not afford to purchase commercial floor coverings. Rugs were made for one's own home, and only rarely sold. Most of these householders were completely untrained in the arts, and unless they had (as only a few did) an innate creative sense, they relied for inspiration upon standard commercial patterns.

Around 1900, however, a new sort of craftsman entered the field. This was the educated, well-to-do city person, usually a summer visitor, who discovered the craft, recognized its inherent business possibilities, and proceeded to set up a small but organized group of rug makers with a more or less common style. This had never been done before. Although there was a vague tradition of "rug frolics," comparable to quilting bees, rug making heretofore had always been done by isolated individuals.

One of the first of this new breed of rug maker was Mrs. Helen Albee, a designer who settled in Pequaket, New Hampshire, in 1899. Interested in local hooked textiles, she created some patterns with colors more restrained than was the custom, and had them made up by women in the community. As these sold well, Mrs. Albee expanded her operation, making stencils, dyeing cloth, and training some 30 local workers in the craft. She also promoted the floor coverings produced, arranging for their exhibition and sale, and establishing a viable trade that flourished for some years. Textiles from this center were always marked "An Abenakee Rug," referring to the neighborhood in which they were manufactured.

Likewise, in Center Lovell, Maine, Mrs. Douglas Volk, wife of a well-known painter, organized a small group of craftspeople in 1900 to produce all-wool rugs from a pattern she designed and called the Sabatos. This group used locally produced wool—carded, spun, and dyed on the spot. The finished products were sold throughout New England.

In 1902 Lucy D. Thomson organized another such center. This one, located in Belchertown, Massachusetts, marketed the so-called Subbekashe rugs, which were inspired by American Indian motifs.

In the early years of the twentieth century, other, similar groups appeared across the country. The lonely Cranberry Isles, off the Maine coast, ran a small industry for a time. All rugs made there were marked "CR." In the 1920's the Cranberry Isles idea was expanded through the efforts of the Maine Seacoast Missionary Society. An official of this organization, Mrs. Alice Peasley, encouraged isolated island women to make textiles that were then marketed by the Society.

The South End Settlement House of Boston, Massachusetts,

established a hooked-rug business in 1923. Its products, generally oblong in shape, were dyed and carefully made on the premises, and then exhibited and sold in Boston, New York, and other major cities.

In the South, Rosemont Industries was established in 1920 in Marion, Virginia. Organized by the Farm Bureau and later run by Mrs. Laura Copenhaver, Rosemont was perhaps the most prolific source of hooked rugs in the area. The patterns employed, though based on traditional themes, were for the most part created by Mrs. Copenhaver. Rosemont always used wool that was obtained from local sheep herders and hand dyed in neighboring farmhouses.

Another southern center was the "Spinning Wheel," a handicraft cooperative founded in 1923 in Asheville, North Carolina, by Clementine Douglas. There, rug making was encouraged as a means, in the founder's words, ". . . of adapting mountain industries to these changing times." While offering some guidance in design, the group's instructors were generally quite willing to leave the creative initiative to the numerous mountain families who made and then marketed their textiles through the organization. Another leading rug-making center in this region was the Carcassone Community House at Gander, Kentucky, established in 1925.

During the 1920's and 1930's, rug hooking became one of the several crafts upon which Appalachian Mountain families relied to sustain themselves when farming, logging, and other traditional sources of income dwindled in the face of, first, technological advances, and then a crushing depression. That this kind of enterprise was successful is attested to by the fact that in 1930 alone, one group, the Apison Community Rug Makers of Hamilton County, Tennessee, sold no less than $10,000 worth of floor coverings.

The revival in rug hooking was not confined to organized groups. Individuals continued, as they do today, to work independently. In 1934, the first National Hooked-Rug Exhibit was held in West Springfield, Massachusetts, and the more than 500 entries represented every state in the Union. *Woman's Day* magazine ran national hooked-rug competitions throughout the 1930's, and this periodical, as well as others, such as *Life* and *The Christian Science Monitor*, frequently featured photographs of contemporary hooked textiles.

Rug making began to decline during the Second World War, when, for the first time, women entered the work force in large numbers. During the postwar period, the general prosperity and influx of cheap foreign carpets threatened the death knell for the old craft. But once more it rose from obscurity. The 1970's have seen a vastly increased interest in rug making as well as in other handicrafts. To propagate their craft and share experiences, serious devotees have organized clubs and issued publications such as *The Rug Hooker*. Photographs of hooked textiles are once more appearing in national magazines, and various types of exhibits are being organized around the country. It seems safe to say that the ancient art of rug hooking is alive and well in modern, plastic America.

FLORAL RUGS

Without question, rugs dominated by floral motifs have been—and still are—the most popular among rug makers, if not among collectors. The Bedd Ruggs of New England, the earliest rugs of which we have any knowledge, are florals; one of these, illustrated in Kent's *The Hooked Rug*, bears the date 1782.

That the employment of design elements such as flowers, vines, and leaves should have had such wide acceptance among early workers is understandable. New England and eastern Canada, the true home of the hooked rug, have long, cold winters. It is only natural that the farmwife should have chosen to brighten her dimly lit home with floor coverings whose patterns recalled the bright colors and warm days of an all-too-brief growing season. Such a preference, once established, was reinforced by the relative ease with which flowers could be drawn, the influence of floral-based European carpets, and, later on, by the preference shown for such motifs by commercial rug-pattern manufacturers such as Frost and Garrett.

Representational Florals

Floral rugs may be generally divided into two categories—those in which the worker attempted to achieve an accurate representation of identifiable plants, and those in which floral motifs are abstracted or distorted to achieve a design effect often little related to the original source of inspiration. The former, frequently termed natural or realistic, are the oldest and most common.

Older specimens are made of homespun and woven linen and are characterized by delicate vine- or rope-work borders and by realistic sprays and wreaths of flowers. Often these were set down without thought of a formal design. Details, as you can see from the example illustrated on page 135, tend to be extremely elaborate. The artisans were so precise that it is often possible to recognize specific flowers. The most popular flowers seem to have been lilies, hollyhocks, daisies, pansies, roses, harebells, heartsease, and, especially in Pennsylvania, tulips.

Two distinct lines of development may be seen in such floral rugs. In New England and the English-speaking provinces of eastern Canada, hooked bed rugs and floor coverings tended at first to be almost entirely asymmetrical. Examples from the late eighteenth or early nineteenth centuries are decorated with either a multitude of casually placed floral nosegays or an uncentered vine-form pattern that meanders aimlessly but charmingly across the surface. Individual flowers are small and carefully worked and bear a distinct resemblance to those found on contemporary crewel work.

In fact, crewel may well be the major source of inspiration for such rugs. Crewel is a form of yarn work in which flower and leaf devices are based on recognizable plants such as the English rose, the thistle, and the carnation. These are often used in combination with Oriental motifs taken from Chinese porcelains and East Indian cotton prints. Work in this manner was well known during the 1700's, and a great deal of it was brought to the American colonies.

As the nineteenth century advanced, rugs of this unbalanced and extremely individualistic nature became less and less common. Later examples of this type of design seem to have originated in remote areas where the new commercial patterns were not readily available.

Lack of symmetry, however, does not necessarily indicate a limited knowledge of the more balanced, modern forms. It may well have been a matter of personal choice. Floor coverings of this type are often made of commercial yarns and stained with twentieth-century industrial dyes. A worker with these materials available to her was not likely to be unfamiliar with contemporary patterns. She simply preferred not to use them. Some of these mats are among the most interesting of all available. Sophisticated collectors seek them out, and can readily distinguish these specimens, not only from pattern-based rugs, but from those simply influenced by patterns or other outside sources.

In French Canada, the Acadians have for many years created complex designs with generally symmetrical units based on floral motifs. While the compositions vary, they typically consist of a central figure such as a bouquet or basket of flowers surrounded by a vine-form or floral border. In the earlier mats, such as the splendid piece illustrated on page 135, the border is worked in great detail and contains many recognizable leaves and flowers. Later rugs (see page 106) employ less realistic vinelike scrollwork, sprays, and ribbons. These are clearly adaptations of designs common to the Aubusson, Moquette, and Savonnaire floor coverings, which were made in Europe and imported to Canada in substantial quantities during the eighteenth and nineteenth centuries.

The Acadians also developed and employed the technique of embossing or "hoving up" a portion, usually the center, of a rug by hooking it higher than the foundation, or by trimming the foundation to create a relief effect. In the rug shown on page 56, the dog is raised substantially above the surrounding background. When used in moderation, this method is an interesting novelty. When overdone (as in some later floor coverings in which the central area might stand as much as three inches higher than the rest of the rug), it can result in some nasty falls. "Hoving up" spread into other areas, such as Nova Scotia, Prince Edward Island, and even New Hampshire, but it is always thought of as a peculiarly Acadian device. Since it involves more than the ordinary amount of time and skill, the technique was not used very often.

It is probably to the Acadian designs that most Victorian and later rug patterns may be traced. With the passage of time, the motifs became simplified and somewhat stylized, though they continued to bear the mark of their origin. Vinework was replaced with rope or scrollwork; leaves became less complex; and the rug was dominated by a standardized basket of flowers. What Kent calls the "Jardinière Mat" became an accepted standard. The colors, though somewhat modified by changes in technology, also remained amazingly consistent. Where the early New England floor coverings used subtle colors and more subtle variations—due partially to the use of natural dyes and partially to preference—the Canadian specimens emphasized bold hues. During the later nineteenth century these became more pronounced and were frequently accompanied by glaring contrasts. Heavy black borders began to appear, and these were often accompanied by bright pinks, oranges, and blues against a stark white ground.

These developments, of course, coincided with the introduction of chemical colors and mass-produced patterns, but they also reflected the general deterioration in craft design that accompanied the rise of American industrialization between 1850 and 1900.

No discussion of florals can omit an examination of the standard floral patterns. A hundred years ago, as today, these were the source of inspiration of most rug makers. To say, as Kent does, that they were universally bad is to overstate the case. True, some were execrable, but many were decently done, and the early specimens, especially, had a charm that is quite appealing. Still, it is admittedly difficult to admire a design that, like Frost's Number 60, is described as having ". . . a corner of red and moss rose with leaves, birds, & separated by a pretty scroll from a very handsome and delicately shaded centre of flowers."

These stamped-pattern rugs are readily recognizable by their rigid and somewhat mechanical scrollwork as well as by a consistent symmetry. Generally, if both ends of a mat are identical in design, as in the examples pictured on pages 25 and 157, one may safely conclude that they were taken from a standard design. Many of these (see, for example, page 156) were essentially borders with a large empty space in the center to allow the rugmaker to incorporate other devices either from stock patterns or of her own creation. In *Handmade Rugs*, Ella Bowles gives us an interesting insight into the origins of many of these central figures. When she once asked an elderly woman about her sources of inspiration, she received the following response:

I made lots o' horn-o-plenty rugs when I was a young girl. Would you like to know how I marked off my designs? I laid a piece of paper down on a horn-o-plenty someone had hooked in a rug and pricked over the design with a needle. Then I took a piece of burnt wood and rubbed over the holes, and my pattern would show on my foundation.

Such an explanation goes a long way toward explaining the combination of diverse and sometimes incongruous elements from various commercial patterns. Of course, the manufacturers had templates for individual characters such as scrolls, pine cones, and flower buds, and they could vary designs as they saw fit. However, it is not likely that an average home worker had access to such devices.

The creative process here, as in other areas of folk art, is often more complex than it seems. It is true that rural rug makers were greatly influenced by and dependent upon commercial patterns. On the other hand, these women themselves often determined the very nature of the factory-made designs. Thus Eaton, in his *Handicrafts of New England*, mentions Minnie Light of Burkettville, Maine, who is known to have created several original floral compositions for Edward Frost. Miss Light's technique was interesting, though not unique. She would select flowers from her garden, outline them on paper, cut out the designs, and then trace them on burlap. A similar approach was used by a twentieth-century rug maker, Essie Davis of Johnson, Vermont. She devised a pattern called "Maple Leaves in Autumn," which she designed simply by placing leaves on the backing and reproducing their shape and color. Each rug made in this manner was different, though all reflected a similar method.

The Light and Davis techniques illustrate another important aspect of floral rug development: the survival and continued interest in naturalism. The need for simplicity and corner-cutting inherent in the making of commercial patterns tended to result in stylization and monotony, the very things Kent and other early collectors felt would destroy true creativity in the medium. This has not happened, however; some of the most remarkable rugs ever hooked have been made in the past 50 years.

The development of the arts and crafts movement, followed by the increased emphasis on handiwork as a source of income during the years of the Great Depression, stimulated individual creativity. Far from being content with what is available in stores, rug makers have looked about them and found their own inspiration. Unlike their predecessors, many of these men and women had some background in the arts, and the patterns they created often possessed substantial stylistic merit. Thus, in the 1940's Molly Tobey of Barrington, Rhode Island, won a national hooked-rug competition with the Victory Garden Rug, modeled upon her family's vegetable plot. At about the same time, the Boston Garden Show featured a floor covering called "Rockweed," made by Claire Ingalls of Nashua, Massachusetts, who based its design on a faithful reproduction of the form and color of a species of rockbound seaweed. Numerous similar examples could be given. What they show is clear—many rug makers do create patterns in which nature is reproduced as faithfully as possible.

Conventional Floral Rugs

The tradition of naturalism in rug design never precluded the use of abstract or conventionalized devices, and with the passage of time these have become more common. It is difficult to determine the

Floral: Hooked yarn on
burlap, 27.5″ x 47.5″.
Multicolor bouquet sur-
rounded by tan and gray
border. Late nineteenth
century. Courtesy Dal-
mar Tift and Ilon Spect.

Floral: Hooked yarn on burlap, 32" x 65.5". Rose, tan, green, and black figure bordered in rust. Twentieth century. Courtesy Dalmar Tift and Ilon Spect.

source of inspiration for such motifs. At the most basic level one may argue that country artisans unable to create a rose or a feather scroll that looked like the original simply reduced the figures to a basic form that suggested enough of the universal character of the object to make it more or less recognizable to others. As each worker's solution to this problem tended to be somewhat similar, a vocabulary of forms evolved. These were strikingly similar in eighteenth as well as nineteenth-century floor coverings.

In a more complex stage of development, floral motifs such as buds, leaves, and petals were consciously stylized so they would relate to and eventually merge into geometric devices. At this point one enters the realm of Near Eastern and Oriental rugs. It was the similarity of these rugs to the domestic product that first attracted sophisticated collectors to American hooked rugs. Indeed, some early authorities considered the conventionalized floral to be the most interesting and artistic of all such work.

The transition from simple to complex may be seen in the rugs illustrated. The simple piece shown on page 17 is readily recognizable for what it is: clusters of cherries against a rickrack ground. Geometric influence may be seen in the sawtooth border and lined backing, but naturalism remains quite evident.

Similarly, in the lovely specimen on page 44, the star-like flowers are superimposed upon dominant triangles while their shapes, still quite realistic, take on a rigidity in keeping with the overall composition. The example on page 141, though extremely basic, is far removed from the realistic. The floral and scroll corners are barely recognizable as such, and the bud border has been reduced to a series of colorful knobs with no attempt whatsoever at naturalism. An example of this sort is well on its way to becoming geometric.

A further step is taken in the Labrador mat illustrated on page 00. Here is a true transitional piece with only the conventionalized corners still retaining anything of the naturalistic floral quality. But the overall design, particularly the medallion center, which in a less sophisticated piece would have contained a bouquet or cornucopia, is clearly floral rather than geometric.

Floor coverings such as these could quite conceivably have developed without outside influences. Other conventionalized florals clearly did not. In the 1870's, Frost described one of his patterns as being an ". . . elegant Turkish design . . . copied from the latest and most desirable importations of Turkish rugs, a perfect imitation both in design and coloring." These "Turkey carpets," when good, were very good indeed, as may be seen from the example illustrated on page 62. Colors were, unlike those in many of their more ordinary contemporaries, extremely well suited to the overall design, and the design was superior in every respect. It was, however, no small matter to hook one of these rugs, and they are among the least common in the field.

Pictorial: Hooked yarn
and burlap on burlap,
27″ x 50″. Brown-and-
white dog, pink flowers,
and green leaves within a
blue border. Twentieth
century. Courtesy Dal-
mar Tift and Ilon Spect.

Interestingly enough, later rug makers went beyond these patterns to original sources. In the 1930's, at least one worker, Mrs. Richard Wampler of New Britain, Connecticut, is known to have made direct copies of original carpets in the Ballard Collection at the Metropolitan Museum of Art. Her creations attracted sufficient attention to merit exhibition by the Society of Connecticut Craftsmen.

Because certain of the rugs worked in this manner antedate the known period of commercial patterns, it may be assumed that these specimens reflect their creators' familiarity with imported Orientals, large numbers of which were entering this country by 1850. There is no doubt that many such American floor coverings are made on much the same pattern lines as Eastern knotted mats. They indicate the maker's ability to build up tonal effects through the shading of the dominant hues and to use small dots of brilliant color to accentuate areas of major interest within the total composition.

Floral Geometrics

There is another interesting category, one which incorporates, more or less without modification, elements of both floral and geometric designs. For lack of a better term, such rugs might be called floral geometrics. Since geometrics, by and large, imply lines and angles, and florals are, by definition, curvilinear, the marriage is a difficult and often unhappy one. In the rug shown on page 145, for instance, the severe verticals and horizontals of the block and hit-or-miss border are in sharp contrast to the flower and leaf centerpiece. This kind of design can work very well, though. See, for example, the diamond pattern illustrated on page 123. Here the large floral medallion stands out effectively from a tile-like background. Kent mentions once seeing a full-sized carpet composed of numerous such medallions, each of which had an identical floral center.

In floral geometric rugs, the floral element may, of course, be dominant, as in these examples, or subordinate as in the hall rug seen on page 125. There the conventionalized tulip corners and vine-and-bud border motif serve to set off the large multihued stars that are clearly intended to be the focal point of the piece. A greater balance is reflected in the very attractive floor covering pictured on page 149. The stylized flowers, probably roses, share equally in the composition with the various geometric devices, and the whole effect is strong and pleasing to the eye. The pattern, to be sure, is a common one and commercial as well, for the manufacturers, having seen how well both floral and geometric designs sold, were quick to market combination items.

Sentiment or Motto Rugs

Rugs and mats that incorporate words or verses are not very common. Most of these are floral in motif, with a flower or vineform border surrounding a tablet upon which the motto is placed. Traditionally,

Floral: Hooked rag on burlap, 33.5″ x 49″. Conventionalized or abstract design in brown, black, pink, and tan with brown and umber sawtooth border. Late nineteenth century. Courtesy Dalmar Tift and Ilon Spect.

mottoes were used on the half-oval rugs that decorate doorways. Such entrance mats might bear felicitous tidings such as HOME SWEET HOME, WELCOME, WELCOME HOME, FORGET ME NOT, GOOD LUCK, or CALL AGAIN. Kate Douglas, in her charming book, *More Chronicles of Rebecca*, described just such a door rug:

Rebecca could see the Came's brown farm house from Mrs. Baxter's sitting room window. The little-traveled road with strips of tufted green between the wheel tracks curved dustily up to the very door step, and inside the screen door of pink mosquito netting was a wonderful drawn-in rug, shaped like a half pie, with WELCOME *in saffron letters on a green ground.*

Rugs were inscribed with family members as well as visitors in mind. A promising student or obedient child might find his or her room graced with a floor covering bearing the phrase, REWARD OF MERIT. Religious families attested to their faith with textile pronouncements such as JESUS DWELLS HERE, GOD IS LOVE, and THE LORD IS MY SHEPHERD: tipplers were well warned to avoid a threshold bearing a mat on which was emblazoned the stern warning, WINE IS A MOCKER!

More complex statements are extremely rare, though there is the legend of an old Pennsylvania rug whose frustrated maker had set forth upon its surface the story of her personal misfortunes.

This poor old maid
A bit too good
Condemned herself
To Spinsterhood.
When Cupid met me, I did flee,
I fled too well, and here I be.

Other sentiment rugs were traditionally associated with marriage and were prepared especially for the trousseau. These are discussed elsewhere.

Hooked rugs, for the most part, must be appreciated in light of the romantic tradition that prevailed during the last half of the nineteenth century. Though the sentiments expressed in motto rugs may seem cloying to us today, they express in a few words the faith and optimism that motivated much in Victorian art.

Much the same may be said for floral rugs in general. It took a particular sensitivity to produce so many designs celebrating the closeness to nature and to rural life that was particularly strong prior to 1900. The current renewed interest in these designs may well reflect a return to similar values.

GEOMETRIC RUGS

Rugs with geometrical devices—squares, rectangles, triangles, octagons, cubes, and the like—are of great interest to both creator and collector. To the creator they present the readiest access to the complexities of rug making. To the collector they offer a type of floor covering whose style and color agree more readily with modern furnishings than do the often florid florals and naively representational pictorials. Whereas pictorials, particularly if large in size, tend to dominate a room, geometrics blend quietly with the other furnishings.

Most authorities agree that geometric designs are among the oldest known. Indeed, Arab, Berber, and Moorish carpets from the sixteenth century and before are often dominated by devices such as cubes, rectangles, stars, and crescents set against a marbleized background not unlike the effect achieved through hit-or-miss hooking. Some have argued that European and American sailors might have brought back samples of these textiles which then may have influenced early Western rug manufacturers.

No doubt some such cultural transference took place. Nevertheless, the very nature of geometrical devices makes it more likely that the idea of using them occurred spontaneously to their creators. Few early (or present-day) rug hookers were draftsmen, and they were very much aware of their inability to achieve more than a barely recognizable imitation of any object, be it fish or flower. Even a straight line presented a problem. But there was a solution. The straight weave of burlap backing encouraged rectilinear designs; so, by following the threads of the backing, and marking them off by length and breadth, one might form simple square and rectangular units. Likewise, by working from corner to corner at an angle, diamond patterns might be made. By placing a butter pat or saucer on the backing and tracing around it, one could create a square or circle. A brick offered the shape of a rectangle; the scalloped edge of a serving dish could furnish an interesting pattern, and so on. The possibilities were limited only by the number of different shapes one might discover in household objects.

That this procedure did take place is verified in the following letter written by a New Jersey farmwife to *Moore's Rural New Yorker:*

Yes, my grandmother taught me how to hook. She used to make the sea shell pattern . . . took an old cup plate and lay it down on the material then run around it with a piece of charcoal wood from the fire. She used to lay one over the other so the whole rug looked like shells or fish scales.

Such techniques are still commonplace today, and their popularity at an earlier date is reflected in the fact that commercial rug-pattern catalogs rarely included many of the simple geometric designs. There

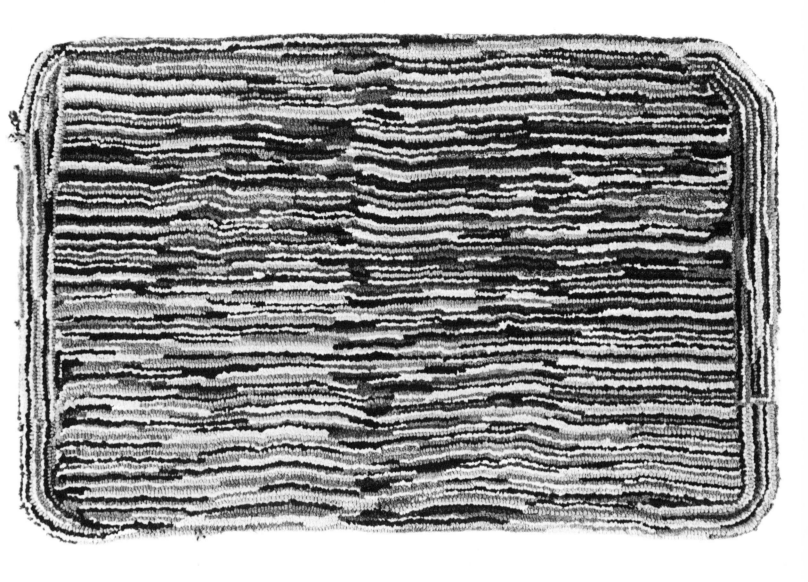

Geometric: Hooked rag
and yarn on burlap, 27"
x 43". Confetti or "hit
or miss" design in tan,
red, white, blue, gray,
green, and black. Such
rugs are clearly related
to the traditional rag rug.
Mid-nineteenth century.
Courtesy Dalmar Tift
and Ilon Spect.

was simply no need for them. Household artisans were much more interested in obtaining the complex floral designs they could not duplicate at home.

The great appeal of geometric rugs to modern connoisseurs is in part related to their resemblance to much modern art; but, of course, the basic geometric patterns preceded modern art by many generations.

The very best of the geometrics, those not rigidly confined to specific line and color repetitions, often reflect the naive artist's instinctive translation of natural forms into elemental design units. These are then reworked and transformed to create something new and different. Ella Bowles, in her book, *Handmade Rugs,* describes how in the early 1900's the women of Maine's lonely Cranberry Isles made rugs and carpets whose design elements were suggested by tide lines left on the beach, by waves lapping the shore, by seaweed, and the tips of distant sails—all elements of their everyday environment. As one of these artisans once remarked, "This is nature's design, and I bow to it."

Confetti Rugs

Most simple of all the many geometric forms is the long line or confetti pattern. At its least complex (see illustration on page 33) this is nothing more than many lines of varicolored material hooked straight across the rug surface following the backing thread. At its best the confetti design has the appearance of a gorgeous rainbow; at its very worst it is still a lovely thing to walk on.

The undulating rows of color seen in this pattern are, of course, nothing more than the old "hit or miss" background writ large. Doubtless such rugs were designed to use up accumulations of multicolored scraps too few or too small to make into a formal composition.

Variations were worked upon the central theme. In one, squares of solid color, such as red or green, are superimposed upon the dominant background, either at random or in definite patterns. In another (see page 35) the design is the characteristic one of concentric rectangles with varying shades of color progressing from the dark border.

While confetti rugs have been made throughout Canada and New England, they seem to be most common in New Brunswick, where they appear as full-sized carpets and runners as well as rugs.

Basket Weave

Most closely related to the confetti pattern is the basket weave. As seen in the example on page 36, this consists of squares filled with stripes of hit-or-miss work running at right angles to the similar stripes in adjoining units. This is undoubtedly one of the oldest patterns, and it appears in many variations. Like the confetti pattern, this design provided a ready use for odds and ends of scrap cloth.

Geometric: Hooked rag on burlap, 21″ x 36″. Concentric rectangles in purple, tan, brown, green, gray, pink, and yellow. Mid-nineteenth century. Courtesy Dalmar Tift and Ilon Spect.

Geometric: Hooked yarn on burlap, 31″ x 61″. Basket-weave pattern in red, white, blue, and green within a tan border. Late nineteenth century. Courtesy Dalmar Tift and Ilon Spect.

In New England the basic basket weave design is often altered by the introduction of a stair-step-edged triangular area of solid hue in one corner of each block. In the specimen illustrated on page 38, the inset is in white, but it may appear in various colors. In another, more complex variation (page 39) the basket weave is spread and interspersed with blocks of solid color. Again, the thread lines of the burlap backing provide a guideline for working multiple changes.

Wave or Zigzag Rugs

Another, similar form is the zigzag or wave pattern in which lines of "hit or miss" work move across the surface in undulating sawtooth ridges. The design is Oriental in origin but obvious enough to be arrived at independent of any outside source. Whether or not the fancied resemblance to wave patterns is particularly relevant, the pattern has always been popular in Canada's Maritime Provinces.

As in the case of confetti and basket weave, the basic simplicity of the wave design allows for numerous variations. Alteration of color alone can be spectacular, with something of the quality of old Venetian glass. Or, each row of zigzags or V's may be separated from the next by dark brown or black lines running the length of the piece.

Log Cabin Rugs

Somewhat related to the wave design is the log cabin pattern, or "Lincoln's Log Cabin" as it is sometimes called. The name is derived from an imagined resemblance to the appearance of sawn logs as they are locked together at the corner of a cabin wall. Since both Lincoln and William Henry Harrison used the log cabin as a political symbol, it is likely that the pattern's popularity dates to the pre-Civil War period.

The basic pattern is square, with each unit consisting of from 6 to 12 L-shaped brackets, often with a solid or speckled center running across the surface in an overlapping design. This rug pattern is identical to the quilt pattern of the same name. W. W. Kent once owned a log cabin rug that measured seven by ten feet.

With variations in shading and organization, a fascinating variety of designs can be made with the log cabin pattern. This design appears in all areas of North America where the craft of rug hooking was followed.

Block or Box Rugs

The basic block pattern is used to make a rug surface divided into a multitude of units of equal size and shape. The interior of each such unit may be treated identically by using concentric squares, as in the example on page 143, or by longitudinal division into triangular sections of varying hues as in the example on page 146. Or, the squares themselves may vary. Thus, in the rug illustrated on page 138 alternate squares are done in concentric boxes and in an abstraction of the four-leaf-clover motif.

Geometric: Hooked rag on
burlap, 35" x 41". Saw-
tooth or stairstep pattern
in gray, white, red, tan,
black, and blue. Late
nineteenth century. Cour-
tesy Dalmar Tift and Ilon
Spect.

Geometric: Hooked rag on
burlap, 33" x 33". Open-
work basket weave in blue,
tan, and pink. Late nine-
teenth century. Courtesy
Dalmar Tift and Ilon Spect.

Where done in rectangles rather than squares, this pattern is often called Wentworth Brick, in acknowledgment of a tradition that the first example was copied from multicolored hearth bricks in the home of Governor Wentworth in Salem, Massachusetts.

Inch-Square Rugs

Closely related to the block pattern is the inch-square pattern, which also specifies a surface divided equally into multicolored boxes. In this case, each block is about an inch square. A good example of this design (such as the one on page 57) has the quality of a tile tabletop. The term "tile rug" has also been applied to this variation, as has "Boston Sidewalk," in honor of some fancied resemblance to the early brick walkways of that city.

When bold colors are applied in an imaginative way, as in the quilt-like rug seen on page 54, the inch-square design reflects a creative power that transcends the extremely simple structural concept.

While done elsewhere as well, this pattern is traditionally associated with the rug makers of New England and eastern Canada, particularly New Brunswick and the Maine coast, where quilts and floor coverings in nearly identical designs are often found in the same home.

Cross-Pattern Rugs

An extension of the basic box, cross-pattern designs have always been popular, especially along the Atlantic coast. There are two major variations, the first of which is the Germanic cross, a simple four-legged device. The example on page 151 is unusually interesting as a bridging piece, incorporating elements generally associated with other styles. Thus, the boxes alternating with the cross are laid out in confetti work, while the background consists of an inch-square grid.

The stepped, or Maltese, cross is more challenging and more effective as an art form. In the example illustrated on page 43, the lighter and more abstract crosses are superimposed upon a background of darker rectangles. Together they create a powerful and fluid composition.

In the rug on page 41, on the other hand, the old inch-square pattern is worked up as a part of, and as a background for, a single massive Maltese cross that completely dominates the center of the work. In the specimen shown on page 143 the grid pattern is effectively abandoned, and the crosses range up and down the length and breadth of the surface in a multitude of forms and color gradations. The possibilities seem endless, and endlessly exciting. Small wonder that the cross has been a favorite for at least a hundred years, from Florida to Maine and on into the Canadian provinces.

Diamond and Latticework Rugs

As previously mentioned, one of the more common and easier ways to create a rug pattern is to hook diagonally from corner to corner.

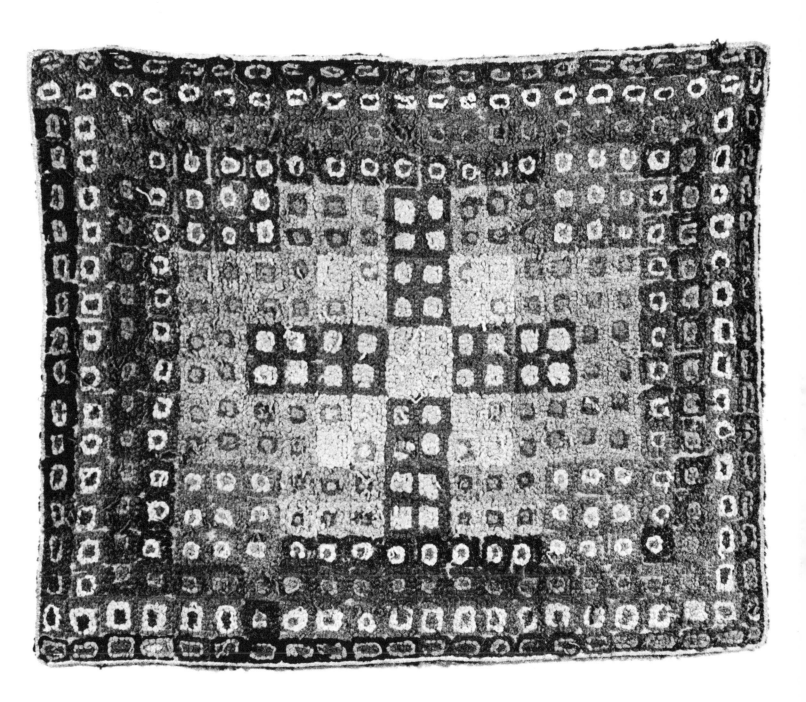

Geometric: Hooked rag on
burlap, 28″ x 34″. Inch-
square and cross pattern in
brown, red, blue, gray, and
yellow. Mid-nineteenth
century. Courtesy Dalmar
Tift and Ilon Spect.

The result is the well-known diamond pattern that is so popular in full-sized carpets. As with the various box patterns, interesting color combinations solve the problem of monotony that is inherent in the design.

A variation is the lattice, or trellis, pattern. This has not been as popular as the diamond pattern or other standard geometric designs. Nevertheless, inasmuch as it was among the stamped "store-bought" designs distributed by commercial pattern makers such as Frost, it is frequently seen.

The basic structure of this pattern consists of lines or sticks crossed at an acute angle as in the diamond device, but in a more open form to allow for the interspersing of other motifs. Usually, small flowers are used as in the so-called Watson Diamond, a traditional Canadian pattern. The extended quality of this design makes it particularly suitable for stair runners, and one of these recently exhibited at New York City's Museum of American Folk Art was no less than 17 feet long.

Color-filled diamond or lattice work frequently appears as bordering material on floral or pictorial rugs. The familiar sawtooth edging (see page 44) is a good example.

Shell or Fish-Scale Rugs

Given the nature of the backing material, it is not surprising that curvilinear geometrics are less common than those worked on variations of the straight line. Nevertheless, there are several such designs. The most popular and probably the oldest is the shell or fish scale. This is an imbricated design found both as pattern and ground on rugs from New Brunswick, Prince Edward Island, and eastern Maine. There is a tradition that the shell design was taken to Prince Edward Island by an English minister, but the motif is far too old to be traced to so relatively recent a source.

As may be seen in the example on page 55, the design of overlapping arcs could easily be achieved by tracing around a plate or cup, and the variation of hue could result in an extremely effective pattern.

A variant of the shell device is often used as a mat border, with the rounded top of the shell pointing into the center of the piece from which it usually varies considerably in tone or color. The part of the design that is somewhat attenuated is called "lamb's tongue."

Pie-Plate Rugs

The interesting pie plate design on the cover is, of course, closely related to the fish scale. A series of connected and interrelated circles is broken into individual units of color, thereby creating a bold kaleidoscopic effect. Such rugs have much the same quality as a crazy quilt. Indeed, Eaton* describes a type known as the "broken dish," which

* Eaton, Allen H. *Handicrafts of the Southern Highlands* Dover Publication, Inc. 1973.

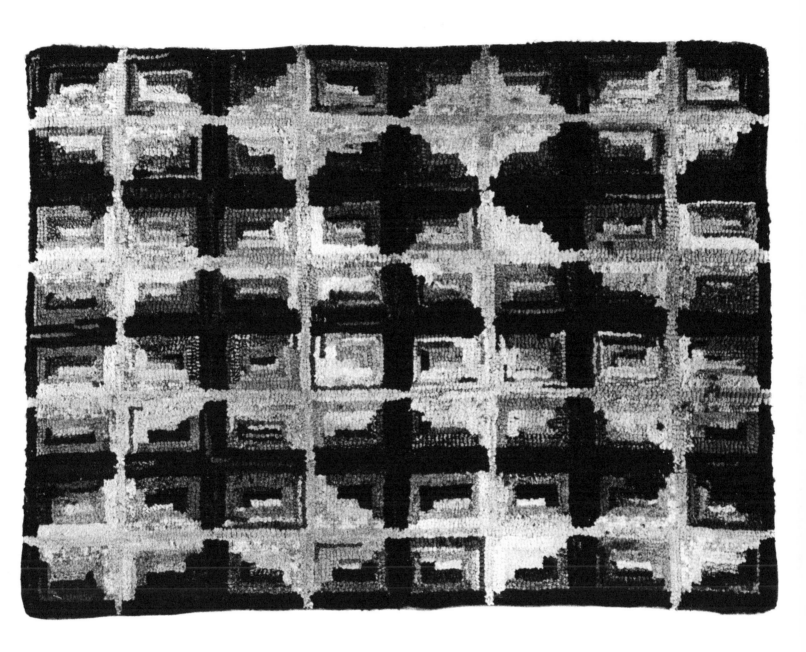

Geometric: Hooked rag
and yarn on burlap,
25.5″ x 35.5″. Maltese
Cross pattern in pink,
red, white, blue, and
gray. Late nineteenth
century. Courtesy Dal-
mar Tift and Ilon Spect.

Floral-Geometric: Hooked
rag on burlap, 28" x 39.5".
Stylized green leaves and
flowers on blue-black
ground with sawtooth
border in gray and tan.
Late nineteenth century.
Courtesy Dalmar Tift and
Ilon Spect.

was made by the Abbott family of Eliot, Maine, and which probably came from just such a source.

As in the case of the shell rugs, inspiration for this basic design was always available in the pantry or china closet. Color choice is particularly important in these pieces, for without sound judgment in this regard the rug breaks down into a jumble of unrelated forms.

Miscellaneous Geometric Rugs

Entire rugs have also been created from repetitions of other geometric devices, such as the Greek key, the star, the hexagon, and the octagon. The star, particularly one with four points (which was related to the German cross), was most popular. This pattern, which was not especially difficult to work, was a readily recognizable and much-approved symbol. The striking design used in the how-to section of this book is another variation. Here, an 8-armed star has been visualized as a compass, with remarkable color contrasts and background flow. The design seems to be unique if not very old.

It is in these free-form or nonpatterned geometrics that the finest work is often achieved. The artist extracts symbols from her environment and modifies and rearranges them in forms that reflect her own taste.

Sources of such inspiration are often difficult to determine. The rug shown on page 119 seems distinctly related to Indian textiles of the American Southwest, and may well reflect its creator's familiarity with Zuñi or Navajo blankets. The rolling color flourishes of the piece on page 155 are less easily identified. Its similarity to certain forms of modern abstract art is, however, quite clear.

In other examples, the design has a more easily recognizable source. The rope-like pattern known as New England Twist is probably related to the carving on Tudor furniture. A narrower variation used with nautical subjects is clearly intended to represent a ship's lines or anchor chain. Arrowhead devices have an obvious source in the New England past. Speculation as to origins of hooked rug designs can go on endlessly, as in most other areas of American folk art. Ultimately, however, one must deal directly with the object itself and whether or not it works as an artistic creation. At that point one may say that the abstract geometrics do work most effectively.

PICTORIAL RUGS

There is a wide variety of pictorial rugs. These run all the way from simple arrangements of objects such as anchors, stars, and the like, to complex landscapes. Pictorial motifs do not seem to have been favored by early rug makers, and it was not until well after the Civil War that they began to appear in any quantity. Their popularity increased throughout the Victorian era; and, today, if one may judge from the available commercial patterns, they are at least as much in demand as the traditional florals.

Like the little girl in the poem, pictorials, when they are good are very, very good, but when they are bad, they are horrid. The earliest, not surprisingly, are the best, having a true naive quality of great charm and strength. The early nineteenth-century lion with basket shown on page 61 is a splendid example of the genre. The colors are sound, the design bold and imaginative. A far cry from this kind of pattern are the decadent twentieth-century patterns featuring self-consciously cute children and fairy tale characters.

Animals

Representations of animals are very common. This is hardly surprising, considering that most early rug makers were rural people. The Moravians of eighteenth-century Pennsylvania and North Carolina wove familiar as well as exotic animals into their delicate embroideries, and many New England samples included similar figures. A surprising variety of creatures appears in hooked rug composition. Cats, dogs, and horses are by far the most common. They are portrayed both alone and accompanied by other animals with whom they are normally associated. Thus, a cat may be seen with a rabbit (as in the illustration on page 47) or a mouse; and a dog with various game animals or at work, guarding his master's flocks. The horse appears in numerous poses and may be an unidentified prototype, as on the cover or a very specific horse such as the great trotting horse, Jay Eye See, who was honored in a rug hooked by Mrs. Seth Washer of Morrisville, Vermont, during the 1930's.

Farm animals such as cows, bulls, sheep, and lambs are frequently pictured as are fowl—particularly swans, geese, ducks, doves, and, of course, chickens. An early and splendid example of the latter is the bold cock shown on page 59. He stares at his diminutive owner in a manner likely to cause indigestion in all eaters of eggs and poultry.

While rural wildlife—deer, fox, rabbits, and even moose—would understandably be part of the rug artist's repertoire, it is a little difficult to understand where some of the other creatures represented come from. Peacocks, parrots, lions, tigers, leopards, whales, and even polar bears are found on some examples. But there is an explanation. Most peacock and bird-of-paradise designs come from Pennsylvania where the Germanic settlers used them in a wide range of decorative objects, including pottery, woodenware, and textiles. One of the earliest animal rugs is from this area. It is a double peacock with floral urn center and is dated 1830.

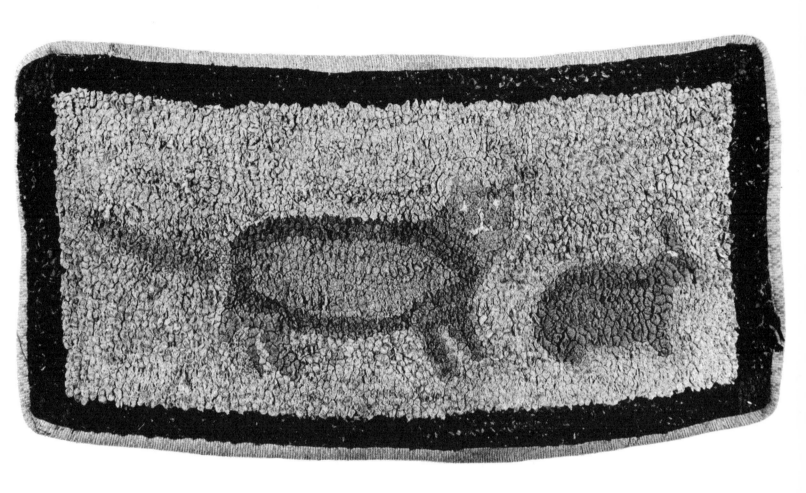

Pictorial: Hooked yarn
and rag on burlap, 16" x
32". Extremely "folkey"
cat and rabbit in pink on
blue-gray ground with a
black border. Mid-nine-
teenth century. Courtesy
Dalmar Tift and Ilon
Spect.

The whale is commonly confined to rugs hooked in the coastal fishing villages of New England; polar bears, as well as sleds with dogs, come from Labrador and the northern stretches of Canada. The presence of African and Asian wildlife can be explained by the fact that as early as 1800, traveling menageries were bringing such creatures to rural areas of the country.

Artistic considerations aside, the most sought-after and valuable of the animal rugs are those with a variety of animals—cats, dogs, deer, birds, and so on—in combination, the rare goal being a Noah's Ark rug upon which several dozen animals as well as their floating home were worked. The time and skill required to produce such a creation makes its presence in most collections quite unlikely.

Generally, the oldest animal rugs are very simple in construction. New England specimens will bear one or two large beasts, usually off-center and giving the distinct impression that they have just wandered onto the fabric and are in immediate danger of departing. Though crudely done in a representational sense, they have a life and movement lacking in later examples. Pennsylvania and New Jersey pieces, on the other hand, are carefully organized and centered, with the animal or animals frequently confirmed within a hit-or-miss or saw-tooth border. See, for example, the peacock on page 120.

The devices a farmwoman used to portray her favorite cat or dog in cloth and burlap were myriad. Elizabeth Waugh, in *Collecting Hooked Rugs*, describes one such rural artist:

"What is that?" one of the authors once inquired, of a modern design representing what appeared to be a jellyfish with octopus-like tentacles; she was collecting rugs in Newfoundland and thought perhaps she had happened upon a rare drawing of some strange monster of the deep.

"A ram" was the reply.

"Ram" means tomcat in the language of Newfoundland.

"But," she protested, "how did you come to draw a cat like that?"

"Oh, us first catched the ram; then us held him down on the mat and us drawed around him."

This story may be apocryphal, though no less an authority than John Ramsey has asserted that rug hookers would, indeed, hold their pets down on the backing while attempting to trace an outline of their bodies. Certainly, the technique had limited use. It is difficult to imagine employing it with a whale or a lion!

A much more accurate picture of the creative methods employed is obtained from the following letter in the *Rural New Yorker* of January 7, 1933:

I have just finished a rug; one which I designed and drew myself. . . . I fold newspapers and cut to the measurements, then place it on the burlap, mark around with chalk, then sew around with twine. In a circle I copied the calf's head which comes on a well-known brand of gelatine. Around this circle I hooked a holly wreath on a background of dark blue, and in each lower corner a poinsettia. These were copied from Christmas cards. I outlined the rug with four rows of black and the circle with three rows of black. It was one of the prettiest I have ever made and I have made 130. I heard of a woman who hooked 150, who made mostly repeated squares with flowers in them like a bed quilt, but I like to make pictures. I am now hooking a deer's head.

In other cases, the representations, particularly of birds, reveal the creator's familiarity with the techniques and devices of the florid Spencerian school of handwriting that was so popular during the late nineteenth century. Form books may have been copied also, of course, as well as popular contemporary publications which embodied much of the style in their illustrations.

And, naturally, many rug makers used commercial designs. E. Ross & Company issued a colored pattern book in 1891 that featured a mat bearing lions and palm trees as well as others with horses, sheep, cats, dogs, and deer. Edward S. Frost also produced a lion design, and both he and John C. Garett sold other, similar motifs. Examples of such commercial influence may be seen in the rugs on pages 117 (birds) and 59 (dog).

Animal rugs, however made and of whatever quality, today remain of great interest to most collectors, and the antiquarian who confines a collection to this area alone will spend much time and money to obtain a representative selection.

Landscape Rugs

The term landscape rug has been used to describe a wide variety of subjects from extremely simple representations of a single house or tree to complex carpets showing an entire village. Moreover, elements from most other rug types may appear in the composition. Animals, humans, flowers, ships, and geometric devices are frequently included.

The earliest of these rugs may well be among the oldest of all hooked mats. They are elaborate, well-balanced scenes, often of religious or historic significance and drawn in great detail. Looking at the dramatic panorama shown on page 58, with its historic border elements, medieval figures, and bold natural dyes, one is immediately struck with its resemblance to eighteenth-century Royal Gobelin and Beauvais tapestries. This is no mere coincidence. Many such pieces have been traced to the French-speaking areas of Canada, and there can be little doubt that their makers were acquainted with foreign carpets and wall hangings.

Far more common, however, are the later, simple representations of home life that reflect an attempt to document or commemorate a place, an event, or a way of life. These are often the most charming examples of folk art, for the artisan's need to create was coupled with a desire to perpetuate a specific memory. Thus, the well-known "Blackstone Children's Vignettes," now in the collection of Greenfield Village at Deerborn, Michigan, is, in effect, a family record incorporating detailed portraits of the Blackstone children, their pets, and their toys. Seen thus, it is clearly within the same tradition as the Taufscheine, or birth and baptismal records, that were recorded in rugs made by the Germanic settlers of Pennsylvania.

Other mats celebrate happy scenes such as the traditional Fourth of July picnic (one such mat proclaims around its border, THE FOURTH OF JULY/ALL HAD A GOOD TIME) or connubial bliss. Wedding rugs were traditional for many years in New England, and quite a few have survived. One, obviously intended as a gift to a newly married couple, shows a man slipping a ring onto the finger of his somewhat bemused fiancée, while her lap dog glares at him in a most possessive manner. In the background appear a set of happy parents and, of course, the church. Below is inscribed the phrase, MAY YOUR HAPPINESS LAST FOR-EVER. Ah, for such simple days!

There is a tradition that one such bridal rug served to warm the feet of marrying couples for three generations of a New England family. This example, unfortunately, has disappeared, but others are known. They are usually inscribed with a felicitous phrase such as LET LOVE BE YOUR GUIDE, LOVE PLAYS A TUNE, GOOD LUCK, or MAY YOUR HAPPI-NESS LAST FOREVER.

Houses and buildings appear quite often in landscape designs. The oldest are quite simple and balanced and reflect a familiarity with the composition of eighteenth- and early nineteenth-century samplers. The tiny house shown on page 160 is a good example of the genre. The crude flower on each side of the building replaces the traditional willow trees or elaborate jardinières found in the design of the sampler. A more elaborate piece, owned by the New York State Historical Society at Cooperstown, shows two Georgian mansions in the center of a massive floral bouquet, the whole design framed in towering trees.

The specific scenes and localities represented in some of these pictorial rugs, cannot, of course, always be identified. As one woman remarked while showing her designs to an early investigator, "I just look out the window and draw what I see." Others, though, as mentioned earlier, are elaborate documentations of a specific time and place. Perhaps the most impressive of all these creations hangs today on the wall of the local historical society in St. Andrews, New Brunswick. Done in the late nineteenth century, it is a detailed representation of a local farm complete with buildings, vehicles, fields, animals, and, of course, the farm family, all on a surface approximately ten by twelve feet. Such creations are often dated and inscribed with specific information relating to the locality or event depicted.

Mary Johnson Carey, in her article entitled "Hooked Rugs," (*The Antiquarian*, May, 1925) illustrates a carpet on which is shown the Newburyport, Massachusetts, harbor; and in 1867 the Massachusetts Mechanics Charitable Association awarded a diploma to the maker of a rug, now gone, which was described as a ". . . view of Rockport, Massachusetts, harbor." During the 1930's Miss Harriet M. Cilley of Plymouth, New Hampshire, created a mat illustrating the main street of her hometown. Rugs depicting identifiable locations are, however, extremely uncommon, and nineteenth-century examples particularly so. Fortunate, indeed, is the collector who acquires one.

Most rugs in this category are oblong or rectangular. A few are entrance mats and fewer still are stair runners. So-called "pictorial" stair runners were made during the first years of the twentieth century. The treads are plain hit-or-miss, and the risers are decorated with pictures of houses, humans, and animals. At a distance they can create a spectacular panorama of line and color.

One of the most charming and significant aspects of landscape rugs is that their very free-hand character has inhibited the use of standard-factory produced designs. While such patterns do exist (see illustration on page 112), commercial landscapes have probably been used less than any other commercial designs. Far more often, the rug was the product of the maker's imagination coupled with her observation of a familiar scene.

Nautical Rugs

Though confined originally to coastal areas, nautical rugs and carpets have become popular throughout Canada and the United States. The oldest probably do not antedate the 1870's, but a very substantial number were made during the last century. They are basically of two types: those depicting individual sailing ships of various sorts and those using nautical paraphernalia such as cables, harpoons, anchors, signal flags, tridents, fish, waves, and sea shells, either alone or in relation to nonnautical objects or scenes.

Rugs depicting ships are by far the most popular. Most are straightforward representations of full-rigged sailing vessels, many of which are identified by a stitched inscription. Among such vessels are the ship *America* of Salem, a privateer built in Massachusetts in 1804 (the rug itself dates from the 1890's), the clipper ship *James Baines*, which was owned by the famous shipbuilder David McKay, and the barks *Autumn* and *Mermaid*, the latter of which appears in two nearly identical variants, one captioned OUTWARD BOUND, the other HOMEWARD BOUND. The style and placement of the latter vessels indicate that they were probably based on commercial designs. In the 1930's, in a fully spontaneous manner, Henrietta Ames of Matinicus Island, Maine, hooked a mat that depicted the mackeral seiner *Julia Fairbanks*, one of the last fishing boats to operate under sail off the coastal United States.

There are also more elaborate nautical designs, including a whaling panorama fully 3½ by 11 feet which features a full-rigged ship, a lighthouse, several whales—one of which is smashing a whaleboat—and a small sailboat full of children that is seemingly out of place amidst the turmoil. This interesting specimen, part of a private collection, was recently exhibited at the Museum of American Folk Art in New York City together with an amusing entrance mat on which is shown a whale, a whaleboat, entwined hearts, and what appears to be a falling (or fallen) angel. Inscribed WELCOME, this rug was perhaps intended for a returning sailor.

Rugs with nautical devices are also of interest. The use of tridents, anchors, or cables as border motifs on an otherwise unidentifiable example often indicate a coastal origin.

While one may quite naturally attribute nautical rugs to the wives and mothers of sailors in coastal villages such as Gloucester and Sag Harbor, there is some evidence that this may be the one area of hooked-rug design and construction to which men made substantial contributions. It is known that sailors hooked thrums (short pieces of rope) through canvas to create rough pile paddings that were placed between ropes in the ship's rigging to prevent chafing of the lines. Since these same sailors also spent much of their spare time during long sea voyages on handicrafts, it is not unreasonable to suppose that they may have tried their hands at hooking rugs with a nautical theme. At present, however, I do not know of any rug that can be reliably attributed to a sailing man.

Patriotic, Political, and Fraternal Rugs

Among the less common of pictorial rugs are those embodying political, patriotic, or fraternal slogans and devices. Considering the patriotic fervor of American society in the nineteenth century, one might imagine that rug makers would have devoted a good deal of time to such artifacts. Perhaps the fact that rug making was "women's work" and that women had considerably less enthusiasm than men for both war and politics has something to do with the fact that this kind of rug is uncommon.

As to the patriotic motifs and devices that were sometimes used, eagles, such as the one on page 60, were always well thought of. They appear alone or in combination with stars, banners, and similar patriotic paraphernalia. Flags were also used—the American ensign and those of Canada, Great Britain, and other foreign countries as well. One may also come across the shield or the coat of arms of the United States or of the several states. A shield which occupies the center top of an otherwise ordinary balanced floral pattern is illustrated in the previously mentioned Johnson article on hooked rugs.

Many of the most interesting patriotic examples seem to have been made to mark the entrance of new states into the Union. The best known of these is the so-called "Vermont Union," a rug depicting the American eagle on a 14-star background and commemorating the fact that Vermont was the fourteenth state to join the new nation. Another rug bears an oval patriotic medallion and 24 stars; yet another, the American flag with 16 stars, which, if it is an accurate representation of the rug's date of origin, would place it around 1820. An interesting variation on this theme is seen in an unusual Southern rug that has just come to light. It shows 11 white stars (representing the Confederate states) on a blue background, a small map of the Confederacy, and various other secessionist devices.

Patriotic hooked rugs have been made throughout the present century. Allen Eaton, in his *Handicrafts of New England*, mentions a representation of Uncle Sam created a half century or so ago by "Aunt Essie" Davis of Montpelier, Vermont. Similar patriotic figures are being used in rug patterns today. The centennial of 1876 produced a flood of such items, and the present bicentennial celebration has already had a similar effect. Collectors being what they are, it may be assumed that in another fifty years they will be busily seeking rugs and carpets hooked in commemoration of "the great celebration of 1976."

Even less common are rugs incorporating political motifs. The renowned "Harrison Mat," which was made around 1840 by May Vinson of East Braintree, Massachusetts, is a unique example. In the center of this rug is the figure of President William Henry Harrison. He is on horseback, and in the background you can see the log cabin that was his political motif. Other political rugs depict individual and party slogans relating to campaigns of the nineteenth century.

Fraternal emblems are occasionally found. The Masons exercised great influence in this country during the first quarter of the last century, and a few rugs reflect this fact. A hooked entrance mat bearing the Masonic linked rings device was shown in *Antiques Magazine* in March, 1925. Other symbols of this fraternity, such as the sacred gate, clasped hands, and stars, appear alone or, more often, in conjunction with floral or pictorial motifs.

Patriotic and political rugs are hard to come by. Particularly at this point in our nation's history, their collection presents a challenging and rewarding adventure.

Still-Life Rugs

In the category of still-life rugs one may include any which, though they may incorporate floral or geometric elements, are devoted chiefly to recognizable objects. Jugs, pots, hats, baskets, fireplaces, and clocks have provided the themes for such creations. One of the earliest still-life rugs features a mantel clock from the first quarter of the nineteenth century surrounded by a free-form floral wreath in the New England tradition. The ground is orange, which is used with blue, rose, ivory, and gray. W. W. Kent shows this piece in *The Hooked Rug* and suggests that it was made circa 1800. The generally antique composition of the piece tends to support this estimate.

Another somewhat unusual still life features jockey caps and whips. This "racing rug" was perhaps intended for use in a clubhouse or in the home of a follower of the sport of kings.

Also quite early are the sampler rugs—rugs with composition

and subject matter similar to that of the embroidered samplers that were so popular with young ladies in the eighteenth and early nineteenth centuries. One of these with the typical alphabet border bears what appears to be the date 1784. The numerals are unclear, however, and it is possible that the figures were actually intended to read "1234."

Closely related to sampler rugs and extremely rare are a few rugs that were clearly intended to duplicate the watercolor and yarn memorial pieces that enjoyed a gloomy popularity until about 1840. Kent illustrates one such example in *The Hooked Rug*. It depicts a memorial vase beneath the traditional weeping willows. Other specimens incorporate names, dates of birth and death, and mourning figures. Since reference is made in contemporary sources to mourning rugs used to cover coffins, it is possible that such a purpose was intended for pieces decorated in this manner.

Maps were also used occasionally as designs for hooked rugs. There is one, for example, that shows a chart of Bermuda. The Confederate rug previously described incorporated a small map of the seceding states; and Harriet Cilley, the prolific New Hampshire rug maker, is said to have made a map rug of her native state. This type of design, however, is quite uncommon.

The finest still-life rugs have something of the quality of primitive paintings. They would be attractive additions to any collection.

Geometric: Hooked woolen yarn on burlap, 31.5" x 36". Early blocked triangle design in red, tan, green, purple, and brown. Mid-nineteenth century. Courtesy Dalmar Tift and Ilon Spect.

A GALLERY OF RUGS

Geometric: Hooked rag on burlap, 23" x 37". A colorful example of the traditional sea shell pattern. C. 1870. Courtesy Dalmar Tift and Ilon Spect.

Pictorial: Shirred yarn on burlap, 51.5" x 31". Embossed on "hove up"
dog on floral background. C. 1875. Courtesy Dalmar Tift and Ilon Spect.

Geometric: Hooked rag on burlap, 33" x 29". Early twentieth century. Courtesy Dalmar Tift and Ilon Spect.

Geometric: Hooked woolen yarn on burlap, 35" x 34.5". A rare and possibly unique stylized compass design. Early twentieth century. Courtesy Dalmar Tift and Ilon Spect.

Pictorial: Shirred wool on canvas, 42" x 88". An extremely early adaptation of a European tapestry design. C. 1830-50. Courtesy Dalmar Tift and Ilon Spect.

Pictorial: Hooked yarn on burlap, 21" x 36". Twentieth century. Courtesy Dalmar Tift and Ilon Spect.

Pictorial: Hooked rag on burlap, 37" x 46".
A rare "folky" role reversal in the story
of man and chicken. C. 1860. Courtesy
Dalmar Tift and Ilon Spect.

Pictorial: Hooked yarn on burlap,
29" x 16". Twentieth century. Courtesy
Dalmar Tift and Ilon Spect.

Pictorial: Hooked woolen yarn on burlap, 28″ x 37″. A magnificent example of the sort of patriotic rug prepared for the Philadelphia Centennial. C. 1876. From Author's collection.

Floral: Hooked rag on burlap, 30″ x 44″. A very fine example of an early floral rug. C. 1849-50. Courtesy Dalmar Tift and Ilon Spect.

Pictorial: Hooked yarn on burlap, 30″ x 53″. Primitive lion in tightly hooked
yarn of unusually narrow gauge. C. 1850. Courtesy Dalmar Tift and Ilon Spect.

Floral: Hooked yarn on burlap, 27" x 45.5". An American folk adaptation of motifes common to Oriental rugs. C. 1900. Courtesy Dalmar Tift and Ilon Spect.

COLLECTING HOOKED RUGS

This is a collector's as well as a historical and "how to" book. Of course, the concept of collecting may differ greatly among readers. For some it will consist of preserving rugs that they themselves have made, or that they may have obtained from fellow craftsmen by way of purchase, gift, or exchange. Since a great deal of very fine rug making is presently being done, this kind of collecting is invaluable. It assures for future generations the preservation of representative examples reflecting the themes and techniques popular in the mid-twentieth century.

For many other readers, though, collecting will mean the exciting search for and acquisition of older rugs, those made 40 to 100 years ago. Given the relatively short life of textiles, the collector can quite legitimately speak of hooked rugs made in the 1920's, and even in the 1930's, as being old or even "antique." After all, those of documented nineteenth-century origin are few in number, and floor coverings more than 100 years old (the magic key to "antique" status in other fields) are exceedingly uncommon.

Some old rugs are still relatively easy to obtain, especially in Canada and New England; very few pieces of any age seem to have been made west of Ohio or south of the Carolinas. Nevertheless, because the great interest in hooked textiles during the 1920's led to their wide dissemination among antiquarians in all areas, it is reasonable now to search for specimens in any part of the country. And rightfully so, for, despite the efforts of a few contemporary dealers and writers to create the impression that hooked rugs are somehow a new discovery in the field of folk art (*their* discovery, of course), the truth remains that they were exceedingly well known to dealers and collectors over 50 years ago. In fact, the craze was greater then than today. Thus, in her book *Handmade Rugs*, published in 1927, Ella Shannon Bowles could say in all sincerity:

The hooked rug mania is sweeping the country with as much spirit as the interest in early American glass. You have only to try to collect rugs to find out how everybody is looking for them.

One need only thumb through a few copies of *Antiques Magazine* for the 1920's and 1930's to verify the accuracy of this statement. In the very year the Bowles book appeared, Yacobian Brothers of Boston, noted dealers in fine Oriental rugs, offered for sale at one time no less than 500 hooked rugs, each priced at $16.00. Their advertisement in the September, 1927, issue of *Antiques Magazine* assured the public that the company ". . . will be glad to make selections for you. You can return rugs that are unsatisfactory at our expense. We want you to be absolutely satisfied with what you buy so that you will think of us again when you think of hooked rugs."

Only four years earlier, New York City's esteemed Anderson Galleries held one of several public auctions devoted solely to hooked textiles. Some of the prices obtained then would seem very good by present-day standards. A few examples follow: cat medallion, $40; star geometric, $20; ship, $60; and florals at $32.50, $57.50, $67.50, and $125.00.

It is no doubt this very interest that has led to the preservation of so many fine old rugs. Collectors are much more likely to preserve an antique than are the descendants of an original owner, simply because collectors know the value of rugs and seek them out rather than acquire them as hand-me-downs. Thousands of fine old rugs were salvaged by early collectors. Now, with the renewed interest in the craft of rug making, many of these old rugs are emerging from estates and collections.

Although general interest in hooked rugs has been somewhat subdued over the past 40 years, craftsmen in many regions of the United States have continued to produce them. These specimens too are now becoming available to the interested antiquarian. One may thus start collecting with the satisfying knowledge that rugs are available for purchase, and at prices that, for the most part, are still reasonable. Anyone who has tried to collect early American silver, or even slip-decorated redware, knows how frustrating and how destructive to the hopes of beginning collectors the absence of purchasable specimens can be.

Finding the Rugs

So, knowing that they are there, how does one go about acquiring hooked rugs? Before you start looking, it's a good idea to spend a bit of time thinking about what you want. Do you want any old rug as long as it is hand hooked? Or is the rug's condition important to you? Do you prefer free-form to pattern-copied pieces? How do you feel about color, about florals as opposed to geometrics or pictorials, about possible resale value? A great many questions present themselves, and it is a good idea to resolve some of them before you start your quest.

First, acquire some background. Read several books on the subject. If there are museums or antique shops in your neighborhood where you can look at hooked rugs, visit them and familiarize yourself with the various rug types. Books, dealers, and museums can give you a general idea of what to seek in quality, but in the long run it will be your own taste and judgment that will prevail. Good taste can be developed to some extent, but, like athletic ability, it is partially innate. You have it or you don't. Witness the people, including antique dealers, who after years of experience still pick out and love pieces that curdle the stomachs of most other viewers!

Still, it pays to hear what an old-time expert like W. W. Kent feels to be the key points in evaluating a piece:

The artistic value of the better hooked rugs is found in certain qualities. . . . First, there is in its class no other handmade cloth rug surface which successfully rivals it in mosaic effect, and in knotted rugs of wool and cotton, only the good continental European or the Oriental one offers anything approaching it. The characteristic union . . . of form, surface and color obtained in the wavy free but mosaic-like texture of the oldest, close drawn, unclipped hooked rug is not obtainable in any other way.

Aside, however, from all this there is the bizarre, original, and bold independence, the unlooked-for and unexpected freedom of idea in many a rug which at once interests not only the student but the layman.

Approaching Kent's thesis from a slightly different viewpoint, I might suggest that what one looks for in a hooked rug or other hooked textile is a happy combination of technique and creativity, the latter being what Kent calls "freedom of idea." This will strike you at once when you see either a bold, unusual design or a standard design executed in an original manner.

As an example of a unique creation, "Ma" Peasley of the Maine Seacoast Missionary Society tells of having given one of her parishioners a rough drawing of a pasture to work from with the suggestion that the woman work in a little bull calf that she had wandering about her property at the time. Much to Ma's surprise, the completed piece featured not a calf but a great buffalo, which dominated the entire scene. When queried about this, the maker replied that she had always liked buffalos better than calves, and besides, "that is the way I saw it." The rug sold almost immediately, and there were numerous requests for duplicates.

More than an idea is needed, however. The quality of workmanship is also vital. Too many unusual ideas have been destroyed by the creator's inability to execute basic rug work or by a lack of color judgment. The latter was particularly evident during the Victorian era. If you have any doubts about this, just turn over one of those lovely pastel florals and see, from the unfaded hues of the reverse, what a horror was really intended!

All other things being equal, design is probably the single most important factor in selecting a rug. At the present time, because pictorials are the most popular, a passable eagle, ship, or house is likely to be of more interest and to command a higher price than other styles of floor covering. This, apparently, was not the case in the 1920's when florals reigned supreme. Geometrics have generally been stepchildren, and appreciative antiquarians can, for this reason, often make excellent buys in this area.

The major thing to remember in collecting is the importance of good judgment. Know when to walk away from a piece and when to plunge. Good but not great rugs will always be around. Buy them if you are starting out, then "trade up," swapping or reselling as you obtain more desirable specimens. Buy them also if you can get them at favorable prices, no matter what your level of expertise. They will always be good "trade bait" for something better. But, when you see something really fine, such as the examples on pages 60, 61, and 62 of this book, buy it no matter what—even if it means mortgaging the old homestead. Such textiles will always increase in value over the years as well as provide you with hours of pleasurable contemplation. They are true works of folk art.

Assuming you now have some idea of what to look for, where do you look? Well, almost anywhere. Antique dealers will usually have a few rugs or be able to steer you to someone who does. A dealer who specializes in the field or in related Americana is likely to charge you more, but his selection will be better, and he is apt to be more willing to stand behind his goods. With others it's a mixed bag. One can often pick up a very fine example for very little, particularly in small New England country shops. On the other hand, comparable rural merchants may have mediocre rugs priced completely out of reason, a situation that reflects either their own ignorance or an assumption of yours.

While prices, of course, vary greatly from region to region, some rather broad generalizations may be made. City shops and specialists tend to charge the highest prices. These range from $25 for an ordinary commercial-pattern floral to as much as several hundred dollars for a very large carpet or elaborate pictorial piece. In the country, on the other hand, hooked rugs in fair condition may be found for as little as $1.00, although the usual scale would be $5 to $35. Condition is always important and a magic word with many sellers; so a judicious pointing to and groaning over even the smallest tear or worn spot will often lead to a substantial reduction. Try it, you have nothing to lose, and often a lot to gain.

But shops are only the top of the barrel. Renewed general interest in this field is sufficiently recent to make it possible to find unusual specimens at country auctions, garage and yard sales, and even in junk stores and on the "white elephant" table at the neighborhood church social. Never pass up any "Sale" sign that promises old household objects. Moreover, if you have the personality and time for it, some nice rugs may be obtained by just going from door to door in your neighborhood or countryside. A lot of people have old hooked textiles that are unused or unappreciated, and they are sometimes willing to part with them for a modest sum.

On a less personal level, advertising is often successful. One can go the whole route by placing specialty ads in an antiques and collectibles publication like *The Antiques Trader*, or you can stick closer to home and list your wants in the local daily or weekly. Also, be sure to answer promising "For Sale" notices in these same publications. Even if you can't attend a barn sale, you can always telephone and tell people what you are looking for. They may just have it.

Persistence in collecting is a matter of personal philosophy. Some early collectors like Foley and Waugh thought nothing of pursuing their interest to the ends of the hooked rug earth, even if that meant hopping a coastal freighter to New Brunswick and Nova Scotia in the dead of winter. Well-to-do modern antiquarians, on the other hand, often prefer simply to let the dealers with whom they do business know their needs, then sit back and watch the rugs flow in. For some the quest is paramount, for others the prize.

Preservation and Display

The preservation of any antique or art object should always be foremost in the mind of its owner. In a sense, collectors are more custodians than owners, and, as such, have a very real moral obligation to see that a piece passes to the next generation in as good condition as possible. With hooked rugs, as with other textiles, this problem is magnified. Insects, water, sun, and normal everyday wear all contribute to reduce a good rug to an unrecognizable rag.

Although there are some hooked chair and table covers and wall hangings, hooked textiles were, of course, intended primarily as floor coverings. This means that they have been particularly subject to wear and damage. Though it is doubtful that they considered their rugs objects of art, the original owners of such pieces realized the problem of wear and tried to preserve their rugs in the most practical way. It was customary, in fact, to keep a carpet reversed unless visitors were present. One elderly lady vividly recalled that when visitors were expected, ". . . mother would sit by the front window watching for them, and as soon as they hove in sight would say, 'Sally, turn the rugs while I mind the door.' "

Today, with the exception of mediocre examples, there is grave doubt that old hooked rugs should ever be used as floor coverings. If one prefers to use them on the floor, they should certainly be placed out of the flow of traffic—under tables, against a wall, and so on. More and more collectors, however, are mounting their acquisitions on walls as tapestries or using them as furniture covers, in order to decrease the likelihood of wear and damage. A few are even adopting the Oriental custom of storing rugs when they are not on display.

Storage, of course, presents its own problems. Rugs should be stored flat, if possible, or rolled up. Folding, particularly with older rugs, can lead to cracked backings and fabric separation. Also, since many hooked textiles contain at least some wool, moth balls or other insect deterrents should be used.

Rugs can be hung in various ways. Some people prefer to mount fragile rugs in framed glass just as they would a picture. This may take a lot of glass and be quite expensive. A less costly method is to mount the specimen on artist's board or plywood and then affix both rug and mounting to the wall. Long round-headed pins or nails of small diameter serve well for mounting. A rug should never be glued to its base nor should too few pins be used, as this leads to sagging and distortion of the fabric.

It is also possible to encase the textile in glassine or thin plastic. Personally, I find this unattractive, but it does assure that the piece will be kept clean and safe from inquisitive children and cats. Cats can be very destructive of textiles. If they cannot be trained to leave them alone, the rugs should be kept out of their reach. Dogs are less of a problem, though I have heard of a few that developed an unusual taste for old burlap.

Bright sunlight will lead to fading, and unless one wishes to encourage this, as with a too brightly hued Victorian, hooked rugs should be hung in indirect light. Smaller examples such as entry rugs and chair covers may be effectively displayed under glass-topped tables, thus adding a new and interesting touch to any room.

The question of repair is a more difficult one than that of preservation. Some collectors choose to deal with it by buying only relatively undamaged specimens. This avoids a lot of problems, but it also ensures that much great but slightly damaged folk art will go elsewhere. Other collectors will purchase damaged items and then send them out for professional repair. With the increased interest in rug making, there are quite a few people qualified to do such work. Repair adds substantially to the cost of a piece, however. Finally, there is that growing group of collectors who, rug makers themselves, are qualified to undertake their own restoration.

Regardless of the group into which you fall, you should be able to make at least a fair initial determination of the condition of any hooked textile and the amount of work required to put it into shape.

As a first step, pick up the piece and flex it. If it is stiff, if fragments of dust-like material fall from it, put it down again (gingerly) and go on to something else. Rugs in this condition are rotten, usually from exposure to dampness (remember, some were used as door mats or even horse blankets), and are quite beyond hope.

If your prize passes this initial test look next for tears, stains, and fading. Tears are a problem. You will have to rehook them or find someone to do it for you. Rents can be filled, but only the best craftsmen have the skill and patience to match the original colors. Often the repair sticks out like a sore thumb. Unfortunately, pieces damaged in this way are sometimes so rare or so beautiful that the restoration should be attempted no matter how unsatisfactory it may turn out to be. One thing is certain, tears and, especially, complete gaps in the texture of a rug call for a substantial price reduction. Don't pay anything close to the price you would pay for the same piece in average condition.

More common and less serious than tears are worn or frayed edges. These can be readily restored. Waugh and Foley recommend binding them with one- or two-inch braid. The number of rugs one encounters with old binding makes it clear that this was the traditional method of repairing edges. Kent, even 40 years ago, urged that worn borders be rehooked, and there is no doubt that many collectors are following that practice today. In either case, very satisfactory results can be obtained.

Stains can be a minor nuisance or a disaster. It may not be possible to determine the extent of the problem before purchase. After purchase, every dirty rug should be cleaned. Modern dry cleaning produces good results if the piece is solid. If the burlap base seems weak, it is best to back the rug with linen or cotton before sending it out. If you don't trust the neighborhood cleaner, the work can be done at home, either with a commercial rug cleaner or with a mild detergent. In either case, the cleaning agent should be worked gently but thoroughly into a section at a time, then immediately rinsed out. Don't try to clean the whole rug at once.

Some stains just won't come out. Some rugs appear to have been used to swaddle gasoline engines or for painters' drop cloths. Short of redyeing the material, nothing much can be done about this. One must simply decide how much the stains detract from the beauty and value of the rug and proceed accordingly.

All rugs fade to some extent with the passage of time; and, especially with Victorian florals, this is often a blessing. If too much fading has occurred, however, if you have trouble making out the design on the face of your rug, you may be in for difficulty. Send it to the dry cleaner first; cleaning often goes a long way toward restoring initial luster. If cleaning doesn't help, turn your rug over, remove the burlap binding, and transfer it to the original face. The underside of a floor covering is almost always much brighter than the top: by reversing the rug you give it a new lease on life.

These, then, are the major defects one is likely to encounter in a hooked textile. Most are correctible. Some are not. If you keep the distinction clearly in mind and buy accordingly, you should come up with some fine specimens at reasonable prices. Don't be distressed if you also get a clunker or two along the way. We all do. After all, what would collecting be without a little uncertainty?

BIBLIOGRAPHY

Books and Articles

Batchelder, M. R., *Art of Hooked Rug Making*, Manual Arts Press, Peoria, Illinois, 1947.

Beitler, Ethel J., *Hooked and Knotted Rugs*, Sterling Publishing Co., 1973.

Bowles, Ella Shannon, *Handmade Rugs*, Little, Brown & Company, Boston, 1927.

Faraday, C. B., *European and American Carpets and Rugs*, Dean Hicks Co., Grand Rapids, 1929.

Hicks, Amy Mali, *The Craft of Handmade Rugs*, Empire State Book Company, New York, 1936.

Kent, William Winthrop, *The Hooked Rug*, Tudor Publishing Company, New York, 1937.

———, *A Primer of Hooked Rug Design*, The Pond-Ekberg Co., Springfield, Massachusetts, 1941.

———, *Rare Hooked Rugs*, The Pond-Ekberg Co., Springfield, Massachusetts, 1941.

King, Mrs. Harry, *How To Hook Rugs*, Baker & Taylor, New York, 1948.

Kopp, Joel and Kate, *American Hooked and Sewn Rugs, Folk Art Underfoot*, E. P. Dutton, New York, 1975.

Langenberg, Ella L., *Stitching, Crocheting, Knitting, and Hooked Rug Making*, Holden Publishing Co., Springfield, Massachusetts, 1941.

Lawless, Dorothy, *Rug Hooking and Braiding for Pleasure and Profit*, Thomas Y. Crowell, New York, 1962.

Marinoff, K., *Getting Started in Handmade Rugs*, Bruce Publishing Company, 1953, 1971.

McGown, Pearl, *The Dreams Beneath Design*, Bruce Humphries Co., Inc., 1939.

———, *The Lore and Lure of Hooked Rugs*, Lincoln House, 1966.

———, *You Can Hook Rugs*, Lincoln House, 1951.

O'Brien, Mildred J., *Rug and Carpet Book*, M. Barrows & Co., New York, 1946.

Phillips, Anna M., *Hooked Rugs and How To Make Them*, The Macmillan Co., New York, 1930.

Ries, Estelle, H., *American Rugs*, World Publishing Co., Cleveland, 1950.

Stratton, Charlotte, K., *Rug Hooking Made Easy*, Harper & Row, New York, 1955.

Taylor, Mary Perkins, *How To Make Hooked Rugs*, David McKay Co., Philadelphia, 1930.

Walker, Lydia L., *Homecraft Rugs*, Frederick A. Stokes Co., New York, 1929.

Waugh, Elizabeth, and Foley, Edith, *Collecting Hooked Rugs*, Century Publishing Co., New York, 1927.

Wiseman, Ann, *Hand Hooked Rugs and Rag Tapestries*, Van Nostrand, Reinhold, New York, 1969.

———, *Rags, Rugs and Wool Pictures*, Scribners, New York, 1968.

———

Burbank, Leonard F., "More About Hooked Rugs," *Antiques Magazine*, November, 1922.

Carey, Mary Johnson, "Hooked Rugs," *The Antiquarian*, May, 1925.

Congdon, Ann R., "The Repair of Hooked Rugs," *Antiques Magazine*, August, 1922.

DeWager, Gertrude, "A Memory of Grandmother's Mats," *Antiques Magazine*, June, 1925.

Joslin, Douglas LeRoy, "American Hooked Rugs" (pamphlet). Privately published, New York, 1975.

Kent, William Winthrop, "A Yankee Rug Designer," *Antiques Magazine*, August, 1940.

———, "Three Remarkable Rugs," *Antiques Magazine*, September, 1941.

Museum of American Folk Art, "Hooked Rugs in the Folk Art Tradition," Museum of American Folk Art, New York, 1975.

Phillips, Anna M., "Unusual Handcrafted Rugs," *Antiques Magazine*, March, 1937.

Ramsey, John, "A Note on the Geography of Hooked Rugs," *Antiques Magazine*, December, 1930.

Waugh, Elizabeth, "Distinguishing Good Hooked Rugs," *Antiques Magazine*, January, 1927.

Floral: Hooked rag on
burlap, 40″ x 71.5″.
Formally centered pat-
tern in red, blue, and tan
with a black border.
Early twentieth century.
Courtesy Dalmar Tift
and Ilon Spect.

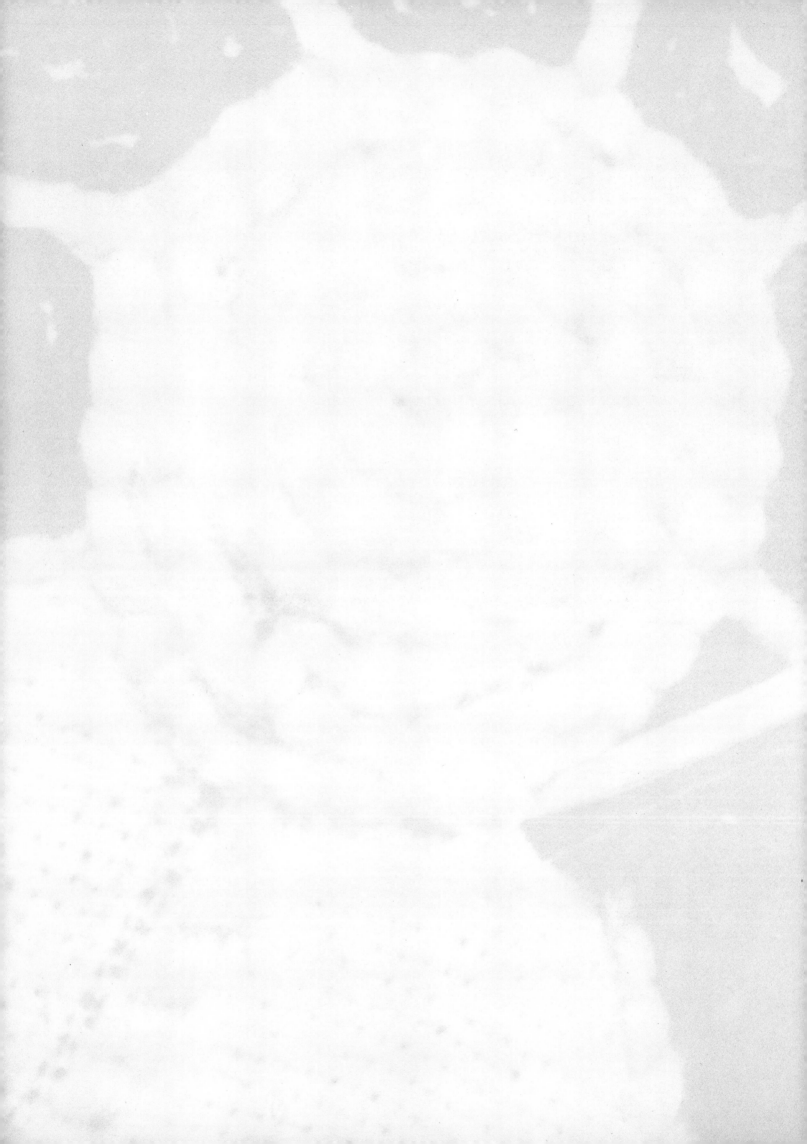

PART II
HOW TO MAKE
YOUR OWN

INTRODUCTION

Hooked rugs are easy to make; they require no particular skill and can be made by anyone of any age or sex. All that is needed is some backing cloth, some yarn—wool is best—or some rags, and some ideas. This section of *Hooked Rugs* will provide ideas and 25 complete ready-to-trace patterns for rugs.

   Before the patterns are provided, here are a few simple directions to get you started and to make sure that your rug will be useful, beautiful, and durable.

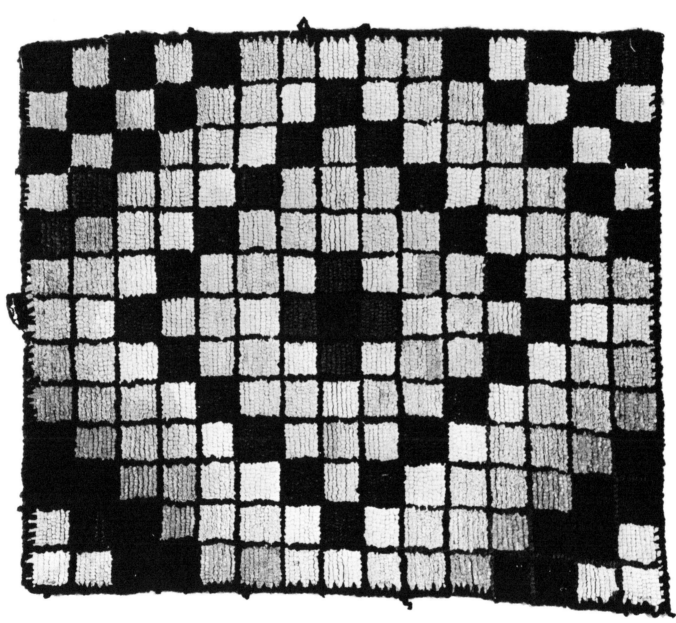

Geometric: Hooked yarn and rag on burlap, 24" x 28". Elaborate block and cross design in red, yellow, green, gray, purple, and white. Late nineteenth century. Courtesy Dalmar Tift and Ilon Spect.

RUG MAKING TECHNIQUES

Whether your hooked rug is on your floor, wall, chair seat, bed, or is made into a pillow, it will provide warmth, beauty, and a sense of history in your home. It can add pattern to a monochromatic or solid-color room or pull together diverse colors and patterns. As an area rug, it can be a point of focus in the center of your room, or it can act as a passage or room divider to link or separate one section of your room from the other. Conversely, it can act as an area divider. No matter how it is used, or what size it is, a rug can be a charming addition to any room—from bathroom to bedroom. By following one of the patterns shown on pages 106 through 164, you can create a truly authentic American hooked rug.

The techniques described here are not traditional ones: they have been adapted from traditional techniques to suit today's materials and today's needs. You can adapt them still further for your own use and your own convenience. Try these ideas to see whether they work well for you, but use ingenuity as well. Invent new methods and gadgets. Part of the fun of hooking is that almost anything that works goes! Rug making is a truly inventive craft.

The materials suggested here take up very little space. You can probably store everything in a shopping bag and work your rug at odd moments—while watching television (do this while working the background only), or when you are chatting with friends, or just relaxing. Hooking can be done with or without a frame. Many people enjoy hooking sections of a rug, or a small rug, on long car, bus, or train rides. One of the advantages of off-frame hooking is that the work can be folded or rolled. Another advantage is that the worker can see that the loops are forming uniformly.

The tools and materials required are inexpensive, long-lasting, and can be found around most homes. You could probably make a rug without buying a single thing. Remember, the traditional rugs were made from leftovers, rags, odd bits of string and cloth, and burlap bags. The value of the rug will *not* be in proportion to the cost of the materials. Some rugs made with only home-available materials, plant dyes, and traditional methods will probably be more valuable and just as durable as rugs in which no expense is spared in finding exactly the right shade of wool, cloth, or yarn. Recycled materials, taken from worn or discarded fabrics and cut rags, often have great appeal. The techniques suggested here can be used with any sort of fiber or fabric.

Lovely, authentic-looking rugs can be made with yarns and materials that are available in the stores today. Many yarns such as wool, cotton, nylon, and synthetics of every sort are easily found in most department stores or specialty shops. By working these yarns with the modern punch needle you can create some of the most dramatic and attractive rugs ever hooked. It is a simple process to thread the needle, rewind a skein of wool, and just start hooking. Using yarn in one continuous strand makes the work go very fast.

Methods and material are only a means to the final rug, pillow, or other item. This book is specifically devoted to North American hooked rugs. Indeed, rug hooking is thought by some to be the only truly indigenous North American craft. The patterns here are usually one-fourth of actual size, but, whenever possible, they are reproduced as large as possible. Look through the gallery of patterns and pictures. Which do you find most attractive? They were all designed to please. You should use or combine the motifs and ideas to suit your own taste. Notice that scale—of flowers, dogs, houses, and so on— is all relative. Don't worry about making an exact replica of a given pattern or some other design. The design of hooked rugs should be created spontaneously. Rug making is a spontaneous art form. Don't worry if lines are not straight, corners are not perfectly symmetrical, or if flowers or animals appear slightly odd: that's part of the charm. Personally designed and interpreted rugs have a special beauty and fun of their own.

Rug hooking is one of the freest, least confining, most experimental of all textile arts, so experiment with size, shape, technique, color, and design. You'll be part of a tradition of American home creativity.

Ideas for Hooked Rugs

Hooking, while traditionally used as a rug-making technique, can be used for almost any purpose for which needlepoint, embroidery, or heavy quilted fabrics are used. Here are some ideas:

Small pieces
belts
eyeglass cases
decorative boxtops
potholders—square or
    mitten type
decorative glove tops
canvas shoes (espadrilles)
bedroom slippers
decorative slipper-socks
book covers
wallets
purses
spats (leg-warmers)
bathroom sets (toilet seat
    cover and matching rug)
tea cozies

Larger pieces
chair seats
pillows
pictures
wall hangings
hats
trimmings
hot plates
desk sets
frames
curtain ties
arm rests
stair treads
table covers
doilies
coverlets for beds

Getting Ready To Work
The Backing Fabric

The fabrics most often used for backing material in rug hooking are burlap, jute, monk's cloth, rug warp cloth, Scandinavian, and canvas mesh. Most popular is burlap, probably because it is most available. Monk's cloth is pleasanter to use and wears better than burlap.

Burlap is a plain cloth usually woven from jute yarn. Calcutta, India, has traditionally been the world's largest burlap manufacturing center. Originally the cloth was shipped to the United States in the form of bags carrying produce. The standard width of burlap is 40 inches. The grades are determined by weight per yard. For example, the standard width of 40 inches weighs 10 ounces per yard, and so forth. The best burlap for hooking has the weight of 12 to 14 ounces. Lighter weights are usually used for upholstery, heavier weights for sacks. The maximum width available is 96 inches. However, all widths between 40 and 96 inches are popular.

Jute cloth and burlap are made from fibers of the same plant. Jute cloth comes in a variety of weaves and weights. Guide threads are often woven into the fabric. Jute, like burlap, is sold by the weight per ounce; the maximum width is 144 inches. Scraps of jute that are sometimes found in upholstery shops can be used as rug backings.

Monk's cloth is woven from cotton. The fact that it is closely woven and that cotton fiber is long and smooth makes this a durable and pliable fabric. Suitable for sewing and hooking, monk's cloth is long wearing and easily cleaned. It is available in widths up to 12 feet (144 inches) but is rather expensive.

Many stores and rug suppliers carry rug warp cloth. This is a stiff, strong, durable, heavy cotton fabric. It comes in three weights; the heaviest weight is ideal for hooking.

Scandinavian is a linen, wool, and hemp mixture. It can be used for hooking, but is most often used for the backing of knotted rugs.

Canvas mesh, a large-mesh stiff plastic or linen gridwork, is often used in smaller grids for needlepoint or needlepoint rugs. Latch hooking, rather than needle hooking, is used with this backing. This book stresses the use of the punch needle technique; latch hooking is not included.

The Loops or Pile

Before either yarn or cut fabric strips can be used for hooking they must be prepared. Preparing means washing, cutting (if strips of cloth are used), and winding into usable balls. Skeins of yarn can easily be wound if you buy rug yarn, but winding strips of rags is a more difficult job.

Using Fabric

Strips of any woven or knitted fabric can be used for hooking. Each strip should be cut on the straight of the fabric if it is knitted, and on the bias, if it is woven. If you are using stockings (an excellent knitted fabric) cut from the top down the length of the leg rather than in circles. The width of the fabric will vary with your purpose. Tight woolen weaves, flannels, wool jerseys, and felts are excellent for hooking. Old blankets, clothes, or bedding are especially good. T-shirts and underwear usually mat too easily.

First, wash any fabric that you plan to cut and use. It should be washed in a gentle soap or washing compound. Then rinse the fabric in very hot water so that if it has a tendency to shrink it will shrink before being hooked into the rug. If the fabric shrinks after it is in your rug, the rug will pucker and look bumpy. After the fabric is washed, remove any zippers, buttons, binding, or other fastenings, and open all the seams. Press the material as flat as possible.

When the fabric is dry and flat, cut it with a commercial fabric cutter. The fabric should be cut into usable strips. When the strips have been cut, wind them into a loose ball, ready for hooking. A large nail or piece of tape can be used to anchor the yarn to prevent the ball from rolling out of control while hooking.

Using a Fabric Cutter

Before any fabric can be used, it must be cut into thin continuous strips. Many people tear the strips; actually, it is faster and easier to cut them. Acrylics and the new nylon fabrics are tough and difficult to tear, but are easily cut.

The widths of the strips of cloth will vary according to how the strips are to be used. Thin strips can be used in punch hooks, but wider strips must be hooked with an old-fashioned crochet hook.

One of the easiest ways of cutting fabrics—and one way to assure even, usable strips—is to use a fabric-cutting tool. This tool is made from a series of very sharp blades and has a crank. The fabric is fed into the blades and comes out in uniform spaghetti-like strips, all ready to be rolled into large balls and used for hooking. Most fabric cutters have guides that can be adjusted to cut a variety of widths, and they work well with a variety of fabrics. Anyone who works with fabric will find the fabric cutter a convenient tool. The bits of cut fabric can be used in potholder weaving, children's weaving, and all sorts of hooking and knitting crafts.

Some ruggers cut in one sitting all the fabric they need to hook an entire rug. Others, simply cut as they go. Wool fabric found in old clothes generally makes the best material for hooking. Some of the most durable rugs can be made from old men's clothing or old blankets.

In hooking you'll want a continuous strip of fabric or yarn. You can sew the ends of the pieces of fabric together, or you can just keep starting new pieces. If you are planning a cut-pile rug, there is little disadvantage in allowing the cut ends to hang out in front. They can be trimmed to an even length when the rest of the pile is cut.

A homemade fabric cutter can be fashioned from a series of single-edged razor blades that are wedged between small pieces of wood and tightened with a vise to hold them rigid. A C-clamp can be used to secure the gadget to a table. You can probably use about four blades at once. Any more would be cumbersome and perhaps difficult or dangerous. The idea is to push the fabric through the blades with one hand and then, grasping the cut fabric ends, pull and guide the fabric to make cut strips.

Yarn

Almost any yarn can be used for hooking, but some types are more durable and easier to work than others. Rug yarns are usually made from several threads twisted together to make a single fiber. Most rug yarns have between two and six different threads, or plies, of yarn. Look for yarn that is resilient, durable, washable, and wearable. There is nothing wrong with mixing a variety of yarns and a variety of textures. Scraps of fabric cut into strips can be mixed with yarn and used for hooking. Yarn and fabric strips can be used alone or together. Old yarn from raveled sweaters can be used, though they often mat and don't wear as well as rug yarns. Many rug hookers buy rug yarns in skeins and then rewind them into balls for easier working. Others hook directly from the skeins.

If you are using old yarn, dip it into a soap bath and then, as with the fabric, rinse with hot water. Try to avoid tangling by keeping the yarn as flat as possible against the bottom of the basin or tub. Hang it to dry by draping over poles or ropes. Because it is preshrunk and can simply be rewound into balls or used directly from the skeins, new yarn is easiest of all to use.

Tools and Equipment for Hooking

So far, you know that you'll need backing material, yarn and/or strips of fabric for the loops and pile, and that the idea of rug hooking is to insert the strips of fabric or lengths of yarn into the backing. How is this done? What tools and equipment will you need?

You will need a minimum of equipment:

- A crochet hook, or punch needle
- A hooking needle
- Some thumbtacks or staples (if you use a frame)
- A pair of sharp scissors

Actually, you can hook with only a backing fabric, a looping fabric, and a wire. However, the work is easier and faster when you use the modern equipment.

Using a modern punch needle is the quickest, easiest, and most convenient method of hooking. Several different types are made. The Columbia Minerva punch needle has been used in the how-to pictures in this book and works well for many ruggers.

The punch needle is a very clever device. The pointed end separates the thread of the backing fabric automatically as the needle is forced through the backing. When the needle is withdrawn, it leaves a loop of yarn on the right side of the fabric. If possible, use the Deluxe Rug Needle, which has a handle with 2 interchangeable tubes. These tubes form a guard, and they allow the rug maker to adjust the height of the loop. You'll note that there are 10 numbered ridges on the handle of the needle punch. If you set the slot at number 1, the ridge closest to the handle, the pile height will be ¾ of an inch —a high pile. The loops or pile will then be progressively lower as you move the handle up the ridges to the one nearest number 10. Now the loops will be only ¼ of an inch high, and the effect will be that of an almost flat-weave rug.

Once you have decided on the height of the loop or pile that you want, set the height by twisting the tube and bringing the slide lock down on the ridge that you have selected.

How To Use the Hooking Tool

As we have noted, the most popular tool used in rug hooking is the punch needle which pushes yarn or a thin strip of hooking material through the back of the backing (burlap, monk's cloth, linen, etc.) and then withdraws, leaving a loop on the top or right side of the rug. The hooking needle has the advantage of being light, inexpensive, and easy to carry. Here is how it works:

Look carefully at the needle. You'll notice that the yarn must go through two large eyes; the needle will often have a wire gauge or stay that will prevent it from going through the backing fabric—and just keep on going. When you are ready to begin, follow these simple directions:

—Thread the yarn through the eye closest to the handle. It should go from outside to inside.

—Draw the yarn through the metal trough and out the eye nearest the point.

—Pull about 1 inch of yarn through the point eye.

You are now ready to work. Always hook from the underside of the backing fabric to the top side.

Hold the needle so that the grooved side holding the yarn between the eyes is pointing toward the direction in which you are working. Push the needle sharply through the backing—as far as it will go. But be sure the loose edge—the little 1-inch extra tail piece of yarn—remains on the underside of the fabric.

Slowly withdraw the needle, taking care that you do not pull the yarn away from the backing. Be sure to keep the point of the needle just on the surface of the back of the fabric.

Move the needle slightly to the right or left and continue the process. Make about 10 loops in each square inch, or, if you are following an outline design, there should be 3 or 4 loops per linear inch as you move the needle around the pattern outline.

Follow each outline and then fill in background areas. At the end of each skein of yarn, or when you change colors, keep the ends or starting tails on the underside of the fabric.

How To Use a Punch Needle Hooking Tool

The most versatile of the punch needles can be regulated to make loops of 10 different heights (approximately ¼ inch to ¾ inch). It also includes 2 interchangeable needle points. This is the most popular method of hooking with yarn.

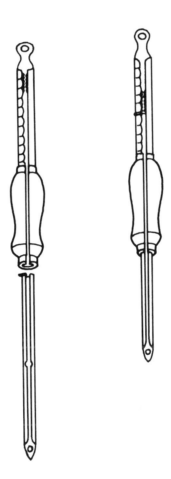

To thread the needle, pass yarn through the ring at the top of the handle, then through the eye of the needle. Apply a slight tension to the yarn, and it will drop into the full length of the channel. The needle is now ready for use.

Punching is simple. Yarn feeds through the tube, forming a continuous line of loops on the underside of the pattern—the right side of the rug.

Hold the needle vertically. For the first stitch, push the needle through the rug backing and draw the end of the yarn through to the underside. Leave about 1 inch of tail. Punch the needle through to the handle—as far as it will go. Thereafter, raise the needle only to the surface of the rug backing, and move the point of the needle forward, approximately ¼ inch for each stitch. Try to keep the stitches the same size, uniform in height and width. To avoid uneven loops, be careful not to raise the needle above the backing surface between the stitches. Be sure that the yarn runs smoothly and easily through the tube, so that the loops do not vary in height.

In the picture on the right notice that the material, double woven monk's cloth, is being held firmly by resting part of the material on one knee and pulling it taut with the other hand. Holding the cloth in this way makes hooking easier and more uniform.

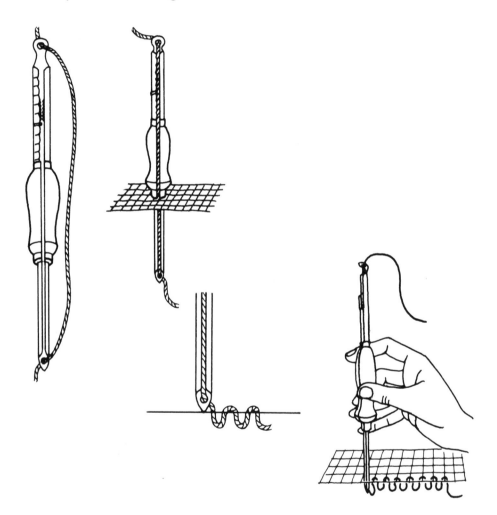

Take care that the yarn does not become tangled as you work. The rugger should keep looking at the underside of the backing at frequent intervals to see that the loops are forming properly and that the rows of stitches are close enough to each other to properly cover the looped surface. You can do this while securing the backing cloth with one hand on the fabric over your knee, lifting the edge of the fabric that is being hooked, and peeking at the underside.

The photographs show the rugger checking the loops on a rug. Note that he has taped the edges of the monk's cloth with masking tape to avoid raveling and to make the cloth easier to work with.

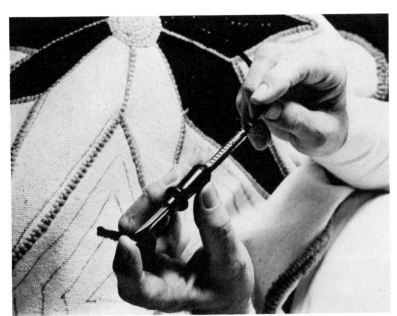

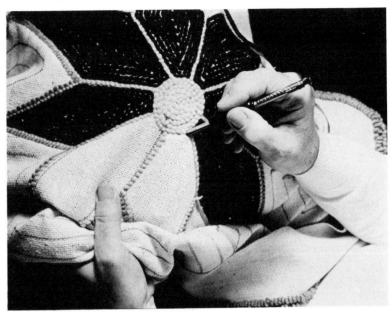

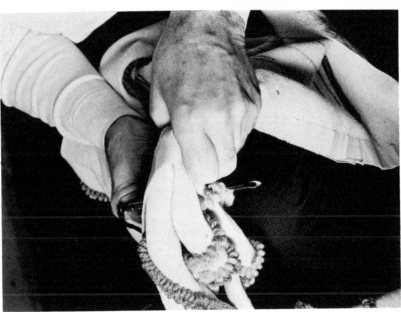

Using a Shuttle Punch Needle

Because a shuttle-style punch hook requires the use of two hands, it can be used only with a frame. Although this kind of hook is much easier and faster for background hooking and some beginners feel that it produces a more uniform loop, the work will be less physically manageable since a frame will hold the rug at all times.

The shuttle needle action is very much like that of a sewing machine. It should never be pushed or forced ahead. It "walks" by itself and needs only to be guided while pumping the shuttle steadily. The tip of the shuttle punch needle goes in and out of the backing with the pointed tip resting on the surface of the backing.

To thread the shuttle punch needle insert the yarn in the threader and work it to the point of the needle. Leave about 4 inches of yarn on the reverse side of the backing so that you begin with a complete loop. Keep your hooker at right angles to the burlap or other backing, and try to keep a steady pace as you hold the handle firmly in one hand and push the shuttle down as far as it will go with the other. Pushing the shuttle down forces the needle to penetrate the backing, and withdrawing the needle leaves the loop. As with a crochet hook or other style punch needle, always work from the back of the burlap, where the pattern is marked, to the pile side, which will be the right side of the rug.

Stretch your burlap on canvas tightly over your frame and secure it with thumbtacks or staples when using a shuttle punch.

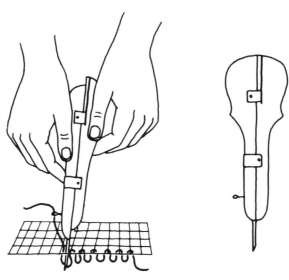

How To Use a Traditional Hook

Below is a picture of a traditional hook that can also be used for rug hooking. You might need a bit of practice to keep the loops even, and when withdrawing the hook from the backing fabric you'll have to twist the hook slightly to make sure that it doesn't stick to the backing. However, it is fun to use, easy to handle, and it gives many people a nice feeling to know that they are working with a traditional tool. Notice that the tool is used on the *right* side of the rug backing rather than the underside. That means that you must put your design on the right side of the backing. Some people prefer this tool when they are making a particularly complex design or hooking letters.

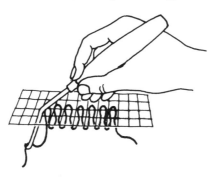

Hooking Frames

Although the hooked rugs shown in this special how-to section are made using an off-frame technique, many people like to use a frame to hold the backing material taut while they are hooking. Frames can vary tremendously; almost any device that secures the fabric can be used as a frame. You can buy, build, improvise, or devise the frame that best fits your needs. A hooking frame is almost a necessity when using a movable shuttle, speed hook, or an electric hooking needle.

If you buy a frame, consider a table style that will allow you to sit comfortably while working. Most frames of this type are contraptions of rollers and thumbscrews mounted on a tilting easel. The sturdier the frame the better. One of the most usable frames can be fashioned from an old card table that has wooden sides. When the center, or table part, is removed, a large wooden frame with legs, just at sitting height, is formed. An additional advantage is that the legs can be folded and the table carried. Old picture frames can be used for small pieces.

You can also improvise by checking in yarn goods stores, department stores, and specialty shops. Art supply stores and art stores often carry canvas oil-painting stretchers that make excellent hooking frames. They are inexpensive and are available in a variety of sizes. However, large canvas stretchers will need some supports because they are not built to take the push and battering of hooking.

You can also construct your own frame. A small lap frame can be made from soft wood, such as pine. Cut the wood 2 inches wide and the length that you want; then nail, screw, or mitre the pieces together. If you butt the edges together and just nail the frame, it will probably be necessary to reinforce each corner with a metal angle iron that can be easily screwed into the soft wood. Either a 45-degree angle iron that sits inside each of the four corners or a flat piece that rests on the side will work. Some ruggers glue everything together before nailing or screwing the frame. This procedure makes the work a bit easier if you don't have a vise or other woodworking equipment. A frame of this sort should not be any larger than about 18 by 24 inches. If it is, it will wiggle.

A table frame is made in the same way as a lap frame, with the addition of a large strong screw that is introduced into each corner of the frame so that the frame is held about 2 inches from the table or other surface on which it is resting. This allows the rug maker to put the frame on a table, back side up, and hook through the burlap or other backing without hitting the table. A bed tray, if solidly constructed of wood so that the rug backing can be tacked to it, makes a very nice frame for hooking and is especially useful for shut-ins or others who are bedridden.

Many people buy frames. Most rug hookers prefer a commercial frame that includes a series of rollers that will allow the rugger to move the fabric on the frame as the work is done. A tilting top for ease in reaching the work is also desirable.

Ready To Hook with a Punch Needle

Now that your tool is threaded, you are ready to hook. Start with the outlines and smaller areas first. Generally, as in all rug making, it is best to work from small areas to large areas. Outline each figure with at least two or three rows, following the contour of the design before attempting to fill in the background.

When changing from one color to another or ending the work, make a stop stitch by punching 3 times in the same loop, holding the loop with your index finger, and then withdrawing the puncher.

Be sure to determine what kind of yarn works best with your particular brand of hooking tool.

Check Your Work As You Go

As you continue to hook, you'll want to check your progress. Following are 4 pictures. The first set shows a rug with the central area hooked. Notice that the hooking was started in the center of the rug.

Always begin hooking the center of a pattern after you have hooked a few lines around the edge of the design to give it stability. Starting in the center also makes it easier to hold the rug if you are hooking off-frame. In this way you are always holding backing fabric rather than hooked rug. The less bulky the fabric the easier it is to grasp, and you will find that by using this method you can control a very large area.

Notice how evenly the stitches have been placed in the rug. This is done by moving the needle the same distance each time, and by carefully following the outline. There should be about 3 or 4 stitches and loops per each linear inch of hooking.

Work each area and then fill in the background last of all. Leave the ends on the top side, or loop side, of the rug to be cut to an even length when the rug is complete.

Here is the same design after the central motif has been hooked and the 4 side designs are hooked. Note again that the hooking always follows the topography of the design. The stitches are very even and close together. The underside of the rug should be clean and neat since the tails have been left on the right side to be cut after the rug hooking is completed.

Note how close and even the stitches are on the right side and how the compass-star design has been outlined by only one row of bright, light stitches against the dark background.

Selecting a Design

After making a few of the rugs using the patterns in this book, you may want to experiment with your own pattern or to combine some of the motifs and ideas shown here. How do you begin? There are several ways.

One way is to work from ideas that are stimulated by the materials available to you. Take out all your bits of yarn—some may be leftovers from other projects—and take a look at the colors. Do you have blues? What about an underwater scene? Greens might suggest plants; browns and grays might suggest an animal. Random patterns often suggest themselves while you are in the process of hooking.

Other ideas might develop from noting textures. A sculptured effect can be created by making one motif in one texture and another motif in another texture.

Do you have any leftover backing? The shape of the burlap or other backing fabric might suggest a design idea.

Inspiration for rug design can come from many sources. Nature is probably the most popular inspiration. Pictures of animals, trees, plant life, animal life, sky, sea, minerals, and the like can often be found in science magazines, photographs, or paintings.

Your name, monogram, a motto, family crest, funny saying, or wise comment might be turned into a pattern for a hooked rug. (Don't forget that since you hook on the back side of the rug you must reverse the script to be sure that it can be read on the surface side.)

Holidays and special events such as birthdays, anniversaries, births, graduations, or weddings can be noted by hooking a commemorative rug. Greeting cards often can be used for the basic pattern and specially interpreted to make them more personal.

Free-form and geometric patterns can be produced without templates or patterns. Series of shapes, or one shape repeated in variations of color, texture, or size, make ideal overall patterns or border patterns.

Historical designs, such as those shown on pages 58 and 60, can be copied, reinterpreted, or individualized.

Hunting, fishing, stamp collecting, gardening, photography, and other hobbies can be represented symbolically for special rugs or as wall hangings.

Remember that when the dozens of ruggers whose work is shown in this book and the thousands of other early American ruggers made their rugs, they often hooked pictures that they thought would be nice, pretty, or fun—or what might look most like a store-bought rug. The ones that seem the most charming to us today are the most original.

Transferring Your Design

On pages 106–164 there are 25 patterns ready to be enlarged, traced, and transferred to the backing for your own rug.

The rug from which each pattern is derived is pictured next to the pattern in a black-and-white photograph. In the color section on pages 55–62, many of the rugs are shown in full color. The caption under each of the rugs illustrated indicates how many times the pattern must be enlarged to make a rug the same size as the original. Although some of the patterns are shown in ready-to-trace sizes, most must be enlarged.

Enlarging Patterns

Most of the rugs pictured are approximately 2 feet by 3 feet. The patterns are scaled so that they can be enlarged to that size. If you want to make a much larger rug, you can do so simply by multiplying the grid pattern and using a different scale.

"But how do I get the patterns shown in this book onto my fabric?" is a familiar question. Almost all books that advise the use of patterns require tracing paper, but ordinary wax paper or kitchen shelving paper usually works as well, if not better.

Take a piece of wax paper and trace the pattern in the book. Wax paper is slightly transparent, so you'll be able to see the pattern through the paper. Use a dull pencil or ball-point pen, being careful not to tear the wax paper. Fold the paper in half, then in half again; then in half, and again in half. When you unfold the paper, you should have 16 boxes. Notice how your pattern relates to the boxes.

Take several large pieces of paper. Newspaper, wrapping paper, or any other sort of paper will do. Large brown paper bags, carefully opened, are durable and good for this purpose. Piece the brown bag, wrapping paper, or newspaper together so that it is the size of the finished rug—about 2 feet by 3 feet. Now fold the large pieced-to-gether paper in half, and in half again, so that there are 4 boxes and each of the 4 boxes represents ¼ of the final rug. Cut out one of the ¼ sections. Fold that section into 16 parts; you now have a large grid that relates to the grid with the traced pattern. Each will have 16 boxes. The small one will show the pattern. Using the boxes for a grid guide, draw the pattern on the large piece of paper that represents the quarter section of the rug. You can then use carbon paper to imprint the pattern on the backing fabric, or you can cut the pattern out and make a template from the paper pattern. To make a

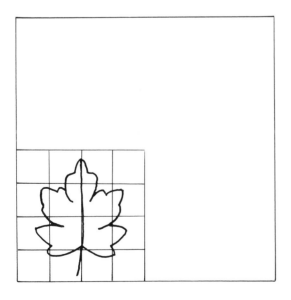
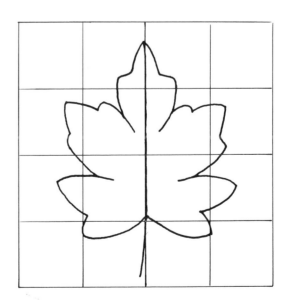

symmetrical rug, most of the patterns for borders shown here must be reversed.

If you want the same pattern on both sides of your paper, hold the paper up to a window. As the light shows through the paper, you will be able to see the pattern and trace it on the reverse side with a crayon, chalk, or soft pencil.

To use carbon paper, place the fabric on a flat surface, such as a table or clean floor, and tape it securely. If you are using a frame, you can fasten the fabric to the hooking frame before transferring the pattern. The frame will secure the backing cloth while you are transferring the pattern.

Pin or tape the carbon paper, ink-side down, to the wrong side of the fabric, covering the fabric completely. Now lay the full-sized pattern of the design that you want to hook on top of the carbon paper. With a blunt pencil or a marker, trace the design, using enough pressure to make the impression of the design go through the pattern. The carbon imprint is thus transferred to the fabric. Pick up a corner of the carbon paper every so often and check the pattern to be sure that you are using enough pressure.

Remove the pattern and carbon paper. With a pencil, crayon, or felt-tipped pen, go over the pattern that is now lightly marked on the fabric. A waterproof, colored felt-tipped pen is ideal: an excellent guide for color and hooking, it makes the pattern clear and easy to follow.

After you have traced your entire pattern on the backing and have colored, with waterproof felt pen or crayons, the outlines of various colors, stand back and look at the pattern. If you have questions about the colors that you want to use, trace the pattern on colored paper (such as children's construction paper). Place the rug on the floor, and lay the paper patterns down on it. In this way, you can get a very good idea how the finished rug will look.

Samplers

Once you have decided on the specific colors, loop heights, and textures you want to use in your rug, you might want to make a "sampler," a small piece of hooking that can help you estimate the amount of material and time that will be needed for an entire rug. A "sampler" is just what the word implies—a trial run or sample of the finished rug. If you make a sampler, size it in exact fractional proportion to the final rug, and then multiply accordingly so that you can buy, or dye, or prepare the correct amount of material. A 1-foot square sampler, for example, will take 1/15 (one fifteenth) of the amount needed for a 3-foot by 5-foot rug. Most hooked rugs are 2 feet by 3 feet; a foot-square sampler would take 1/6 of the total material needed.

Most hookers estimate yarn requirements by allowing ½ pound of rug yarn for about 1 square foot of hooked area. So if you are hooking a rug 2 feet by 3 feet, you might need six half-pounds of yarn, or about 3 pounds of total weight.

The sampler, when complete, can be used in many ways. Here are some possibilities: a potholder, hot pad, boxtop, purse, seat cover, or small picture. Remember that any pattern you hook will be reversed. It might be best to make a circle, or any other design that will work in any direction. To make a circle you can use a plate as a guide or template, just the way the early American ruggers did on the shell patterns.

The Technique of Hooking

Like any other activity, game, or skill, the best way to learn how to hook a rug is by doing it. Take a small piece of fabric about 12 inches by 12 inches, a good size to practice with. Fabric of this size will give you a hooked area of about 8 inches by 8 inches (two inches must be left on all sides for hemming). This small piece can be stapled, tacked, or laced to a small frame, or can be used as is for frameless hooking.

Sketch a small design on the backing. A small circle for a flower with lines for stems and oval leaves will work well. And then begin: Hook along the outlines of the pattern you have made. Outline the center circle-flower and then make another circle outside, and another outside that. Travel in ever larger circles away from the very center of the flower design.

Try different heights of loops, different spacing, and different effects from different materials. Be sure that the backing is fully and firmly packed with the yarn or cloth strips, so that the stitches are held secure.

Keep checking the right (loop side) of your work, and adjust the spacing between the stitches as you work. Ideally, there should be loops enough to completely cover the backing, but not so many that the reverse pattern side is tight or puckered.

Now try hooking the edging. Hook 3 even rows in the same solid color or with the same weight cloth strips. This will form a border for your work. You can then fill in the background with random stitches. The loops should appear to be random, not in rows. A random effect is obtained by following the center of the pattern or an in ever-increasing shapes.

We've discussed the punch needle hook and the shuttle punch hook method, the two most popular methods of hooking. However, as we noted earlier, you can also use a hook similar to a crochet hook, or an electric hook, or even a piece of wire. As you try each method, you'll have to develop the positions for the work and the methods of holding the yarn and cloth that are most comfortable for you.

Following is the picture of our finished rug. Note how even the stitches are and that enough backing fabric has been left unhooked to allow for an ample hem.

Finished rug seen from
the underside. Note how
neatly the hem is pinned.
There are three butt
corners and one mitered
corner.

Finishing Your Rug

Have you considered individualizing your rug by adding your name or initials, or perhaps the date? If the rug is made for a special event you might want to incorporate the date of the original design that is part of the description of the pattern and also the date on which you have made the copy. Again, remember that if a punch needle technique is used, or you are hooking from the reverse side, you will have to reverse any letters or numbers. All dates will have to be checked to make sure that they are readable—that is, facing the correct direction; not backward, when read from the pile side of the rug. You can work these dates, initials, monograms, or names into the design, as was the custom in Colonial times and in the nineteenth century. If you prefer to be more discreet, you can embroider your name or special message on the hemming or on the back of the rug, or even on the rug binding.

After working a rug, you'll want to keep it in shape and make it really serviceable. Finishing touches usually make a big difference in both looks and wear.

The first steps in finishing your rug were made at the very beginning of your work on the rug: the first step was allowing at least 2 inches of backing material for a good secure hem. The backing of a hooked rug must either be hemmed or bound. The raw edges of the backing material must be covered to prevent them from raveling. Place the entire rug on a flat surface—a large table or the floor—face down. Fold the hem over as close to the last row of hooking stitches as possible. Using large pins, clothes pins, or sticky tape, fold the hem back and flatten it in place. Be careful not to fold so tightly that the loops separate, showing the backing. If you have made the suggested 2 rows of loops around the entire outer border of the rug, this will help in guiding you to fold the rug correctly. You might also use a medium-hot iron and a damp pressing cloth to hold the material in the correct position while you work.

Now fold under the very edge of the backing material, making a smooth edge of about ¼ inch. Press, pin, or stitch this edge.

Using a series of running hemming stitches, very much as you would for hemming a skirt, attach the edge of the backing to the backing of the rug. Use a large needle and heavy button yarn or cotton thread. An upholsterer's curved needle might be a great help.

When you come to the corner of a square or rectangular rug, make a mitered hem by folding the corner up and then tucking the extra cloth beneath the hem. A series of small stitches can be used to keep the mitered hem flat. If you are working on a round or oval rug, a series of little darts or pleats can be worked around the curves. Remember that keeping the hem flat is important; a bunch will attract wear and make the right side of the rug bulge.

Hem each mitered edge and dart after you finish hemming the back of the rug.

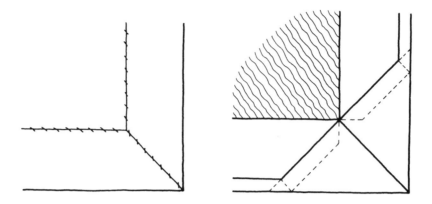

If you wish, a rug binding may be used. A rug binding will give a strong secure edge to a rug, and is almost a necessity if the hooked area runs too close to the edge of the backing. Rug binding usually comes in 1½-inch and 2-inch widths and in natural colors. If you are dyeing an old rug, or planning to dye the rug after it is completed, it is best to finish the hemming before dyeing. Press-on adhesive rug binding is available and easy to apply to either old or new rugs.

Lightweight fabrics, such as linen upholstery fabrics that can be used for the backing of a lightweight rug, bedcover, or afghan might best be finished with bias hem binding. You can find wide hem bindings in most notions counters and department stores. Bias strips of cloth, or other binding materials, can also be used. The idea is to keep the back neat and flat and to avoid slippage.

Latex

In recent years, latex or liquid rubber has been used for finishing hooked rugs. The rubberized finish serves two purposes: it secures the loops on the back and prevents them from being easily pulled from the backing fabric, and it makes the small rugs virtually skid-proof except on a wood floor.

Many different types of latex are available in craft and needlework stores. Latex is also sold in notions counters and in some hardware stores. It looks milky white in the container and is very gooey; some brands have an unpleasant odor. It is always best to apply latex, which is a plastic rubber, in a well-ventilated room, away from lighted cigarettes or anything else that might be combustible. Keep plenty of newspapers and spare cardboard on hand in case of accidental spills.

Slightly more than 1 cup of latex is usually enough for a small throw rug, such as the ones pictured here. If you use more latex than that, you are probably spreading it too thickly.

If the rug is still on a frame, you can latex easily. Place a layer of newspapers on a flat surface. Then place the frame-held rug, face down, backing up, on the newspaper. Spread a small quantity of liquid latex directly on the rug. Using a cardboard paddle or an old spatula, smooth the latex over the entire surface. The coating should be very thin and even. Cover only up to the edge of the stitching.

While the latex is still wet, remove the rug from the frame—a tricky job sometimes. Then fold up the hems and press them firmly against the tacky latex. When folding the hems, remember that the corners are smoothest when mitered. Also remember that the way the rug is left to dry is the way it will remain.

Saf-t-Bak is a nonskid rug backing that can be applied quickly and easily. This type of latex will make rugs highly resistant to skidding and sliding, and it will also increase the life of the rug. This product retains its effectiveness after repeated washings. The latex anchors the loops, prevents raveling, and protects the backing fabric from moth damage.

Here is how to use it: Lay the rug on a flat surface with the underside up, and apply the Saf-t-Bak with piece of cardboard or an old kitchen spatula. Cover the entire back of the rug with an even coat, taking care that all the wrinkles are smoothed out. Then allow the rug to dry on a flat surface.

Drying time normally takes about 2 hours. For best results, a heavy coat is recommended. If desired, a second coat may be applied after the first coat is completely dry.

This latex can be thinned with clear water. One quart will cover about 12 square feet. Since there are about 6 square feet in a small 2-foot by 3-foot rug, more than a cup would be needed for each rug of this size.

The latex must cover all the loops of the rug, even those that will be under the hem of the rug. It is true that using latex makes it more difficult to hem, but one way of handling this is to latex the border that will be under the hem, then turn the hem up, and stitch the hem to the rug. Then latex the rest of the rug and the exposed portion of the hem.

After the hems are folded up, coat the hemmed edges with just a bit of latex and allow the entire rug to dry for at least 2 hours. If you live in a very humid climate, or if it is raining, additional drying time might be necessary.

If your rug is off the frame, or if you have not used a frame while hooking, it would be advisable to lightly tack, or hold your rug firmly in some other way, while you are applying the latex. Taping the rug to your work area with masking tape or bits of adhesive tape is one good way. Cover the hooked area of the rug with the liquid latex, as described in the section on latexing in a frame. After the hooked area is covered, carefully fold up the hems, smoothing and pressing them into the moist latex.

Latex is waterproof, but it will disintegrate slightly with each washing. It will also lose much of its hold when the rug is dry cleaned. If the rug receives heavy wear, or is on a staircase or spot where skids would be dangerous, it might be a good idea to relatex your rug after every few washings.

If you plan to use your rug as a coverlet or as a wall hanging, you probably won't want to latex the backing: the rubberizing makes it very heavy and less flexible. Instead you might want to cover the backing with a light but durable material. A most attractive home-made coverlet can be made with a patchwork of old denim or blue jeans material. A solid-color piece of blanketing can also be used. Any sturdy cloth is good for this purpose.

Spread the backing material over the hooked rug, and cut it so that it fits the hooked area exactly. Lightly baste it down to the backing. Then, using quilting techniques, lightly stitch and tie the backing to the hooked backing of the rug. The stitches will secure the rug to the backing without being visible through the pile of the hooking. The quilting tacks/stitches should be done in the form of an X, about 5 or 6 inches apart. Finally, hem the edge of the backing material over the last row of hooking stitches. Fold the backing fabric and hem.

If you plan to use the rug as a wall hanging or tapestry, you might want to insert a pole or curtain rod on the top and bottom of the rug hem. The top pole will make it easy to hang the rug; the bottom pole will weight it evenly for smooth and attractive hanging. A brass rod, cut to ¼ inch to ⅜ inch longer than the edge of the rug can be bought cut to measure at most hardware stores. Attach this rod to the tapestry by inserting it in the hem and hanging the rug on the wall with picture hooks. This method is most effective, and the rod is virtually invisible.

Cut Pile and Looped Pile

Whether to use cut or looped pile is a matter of taste. The soft velvet effect of cut pile is certainly elegant, and the depth of color achieved by cutting the loops makes many cut-pile rugs suitable for the most formal rooms. On the other hand, looped pile is more resilient than cut pile, and the mosaic effect of looped pile is truly unique. A combination of cut and looped pile can give an interesting sculptured effect to a rug. For example, a central motif of flowers that are cut to bloom wonderfully against tight loops of a woody background would be both wearable and attractive. A cut border of scroll-like lines against a looped center also would be nice.

If you hook one section of a rug more deeply than another, that section might also be treated differently by cutting that pile or leaving it uncut against the backdrop of a cut pile. Early American rugs used both techniques. Cut hooked rugs are especially interesting because of the variety of hues, textures, and shades in the cut cloth.

If you want to cut the loops on a rug, use sharp shears with a slightly tilted handle. Great care should be taken when cutting the loops not to pull some stitches free. If you plan to latex the backing of your rug, it is best to cut *after* you have completed the latexing since the latex will hold the loops secure as you clip them.

Joining Small Rugs and Pieces

Small rug pieces can be joined to make a large rug. Often, rugs are worked in small, easy-to-carry sections to be later joined together. Or, if a rug needs to be a special length or shape, two or more pieces of hooking can be joined to fill an area-cover need. If you are using narrow backing or strips of backing, or if you find yourself with several samples, you might want to join them for a quilt-effect hooked rug. Old and worn rugs can be cut apart and joined to new rugs or new backing, which can then be rehooked to make a one-piece rug.

It is very important to remember that when joining pieces, enough material must be allowed for seams. Wide seams stay flat and work best. In order to join pieces, you will need a large tapestry needle with a large eye, and carpet, button, or heavy cotton thread that will wear well. You'll probably find it easiest to work on a large flat surface. You can join pieces of rug together as you work and/or rework the backings, or you can make the backings separately and then join them all at the same time. Keep an iron handy because it helps to press as you go.

When you are joining just the backing before the rug has been hooked, all you have to do is overlap the two backings so that about 2½ inches of double backing will mark the seam. That double backing can be lightly basted together because the hooking itself will join the backing and keep it from moving.

If you are joining a worked piece to a backing piece, you can do it as you did with two or more unworked pieces. Just overlap, baste, and keep hooking. At this point you should be very careful to match designs if you are working on a pattern that continues from one section on to another. And you'll want to baste carefully to be sure that the burlap or backing-cloth fibers run in the same direction and that the backing cloths are smoothly matched. Again, the hooking will hold the overlapped backing together. Many people don't like to hook through a double backing because this procedure requires an extra push to get the needle through, or to punch through, the thick material.

If you want to join two complete sections without making a hooked double area around them, you must hem each section separately and then carefully sew the pieces together. This is sometimes difficult because the patterns on the right sides of the fabric must be matched; if the design is intricate, this might be difficult.

It is best to pin or baste the two pieces together, or even attach them with a series of safety pins. Turn the rugs over on the right side to make sure that they are aligned correctly. Or, you can align them on the right side, pin them together, turn them over, and do the final sewing on the wrong side.

The best joining stitch is a simple X lacing stitch. Joining loosely but firmly is best. If you join the pieces too tightly, they have a tendency to bunch, pucker, and bulge. Allow yourself plenty of thread and keep going back and forth along the seam, lacing in large stitches.

Because the pile of either a looped or cut-pile rug will cover the seam, the seam will be invisible on the right side of the hooked rug.

Blocking and Pressing

After you have worked your rug completely, but before you have latexed or hemmed it, you should be sure that it is even, that the corners are square, and that the rug will stay flat. This can be done by blocking and pressing.

If you have not used a frame while hooking, blocking might be necessary. Place layers of wrapping paper on your worktable or work area. Dampen the rug thoroughly on the back side. This can be done by sponging it or by laying the rug, pile side up, in the bathtub in about ⅛ of an inch of water. It should be thoroughly moistened, but not drenched. Do not submerge it in water.

Next, spread the rug, pile side up, on the paper and shape it while continuously pulling it even. Two people, or even four pairs of hands, make this easier. Firmly pull and tug, with gentle but insistent motions, to get all the corners square and the edges parallel.

Finally, fasten the rug to the backing surface with thumbtacks, brads, staples, or nails, and allow it to dry thoroughly. For an extra-finished look, you can steam press the pile side of the rug with a wet turkish towel and a steam iron. Place the towel on the surface of the rug and lightly pass the steam iron over the fabric. If you are really adept, you can run the iron over the wet towel, barely squashing the pile, and actually enliven it with the steam. However, many experts suggest steam pressing on the reverse side of the finished rug rather than on the pile.

When making a rug from joined pieces, or when joining a new section to the rug, it is best to block the completed sections separately before joining them.

Be sure to allow your blocked rug to dry thoroughly before using it. And remember: always block the rug *before* latexing or covering the back.

Finishings for Hooked Patterns for Uses Other Than Rugs

If you are hooking small objects such as belts, chair seats, or covers, you might not want to use latex backing at all. Since pulling would not be as likely in a chair seat as in a rug, you might decide not to use any backing. However, using adhesive cloths as backing for small objects can be quite effective. A small purse can be made by backing a hooked section with iron-on adhesive cloth, and simply sewing the edges together neatly into an envelope. A clasp of toggles or loops can be fashioned for closing.

If a small rug is used as part of a bed covering, mounting it on heavy fabric is most effective. Old army and navy blankets used as backing for a lightweight hooked covering can make a very warm and durable bedspread. Because hooked material is so warm and has such resilience, it is excellent weather protection when made into home-made bedrolls and other camping equipment.

Fringes, Tassels, and Linings

Fringes applied to the rug edges extend the rug and also solve many edging problems. A fringe added to an old rug can make it look new; a contrasting color fringe can accent a dull or nondescriptly colored rug.

The first step in fringing your rug is to decide how best to secure the fringe to the rug. A series of blanket stitches sewn to the hem and edge of the rug works well. The blanket stitch is easy and quick. Use the sturdiest carpet thread or strongest yarn available. There will be some pull from the fringe on the blanket stitches. Attach the fringe (the simplest way is by joining a series of knotted pieces of yarn to the stitches) using a crochet hook.

A crochet hook can be used to attach a series of knotted bits of yarn to the edging of the hem itself.

It is best to avoid fringes that are shorter than about 3 inches. Tassels or fringes longer than 8 inches tangle easily and look messy.

CARING FOR YOUR RUG

Cleaning

Although a hooked rug is very durable and can withstand many years of wear, it can be damaged rather easily by overcleaning or by using the wrong cleaning methods. A floor rug is designed for downward pressure. Squashing the pile through wear does not damage rugs as much as does pulling the loops.

If you can keep the rug free from dirt by shaking, airing, and perhaps lightly beating it with your fist or a small paddle, you can usually avoid having to wash a rug too often. A hand vacuum cleaner will also do the job.

Spills and stains can be removed by allowing sugary or non-greasy substances to dry, and then lightly brushing them from the pile. Great care must be taken not to pull the pile. Latex used as a backing on a rug does protect the pile somewhat, but snagging, strong vacuuming, or other pulling can loosen loops, and that is where the trouble begins.

Greasy stains from food, lipstick, or gum should be absorbed. If they are very noticeable, you can wash a section of the surface of the rug with mild soapsuds (such as Ivory) or with less than half a teaspoon of Woolite in a cold water solution. Sponge the rug. Do not saturate it. Clean only the surface. Adding vinegar to the water is sometimes recommended, but usually soap alone will do the trick.

Commercially prepared sawdust-based rug cleaners can also be used. Work the sawdust into the stained section and allow it to dry for about two hours. Shake the rug thoroughly, outdoors if possible. The problem with sawdust is that getting it out of the backing and the pile is almost as much of a job as actually cleaning the rug.

Avoid the use of high-powered vacuum cleaners, carpet sweepers, and other pulling-pushing cleaners. When in doubt, try to think how a homemaker of fifty or even a hundred years ago might have cleaned a rug. The old methods are still best for traditional rugs.

Washing

Washing an entire rug can be done easily at home if the rug is less than 10 feet square and if you have an outdoor area for drying. If you live in a small apartment, washing is cumbersome but not impossible.

First, shake the rug thoroughly to be sure that all lint, dust, and loose dirt is removed. Fill the bathtub with about 3 inches of cold water. Sprinkle on the surface any ordinary washing powder or about ¼ cup of dishwashing liquid. Lay the rug, pile down, backing up, in the water. Then march up and down on the submerged rug with your bare feet. It sounds like fun, and it is.

After several marches and stamps, drain the dirty water, and repeat. After two or three soapings, rinse very carefully while continuing to march up and down on the rug. If the idea of using your feet does not appeal to you, use rubber gloves and pound the rug with your fists.

When the rug has been completely washed and rinsed, hang it to dry, pile side up, backing down, over a wooden pole, or lay it, pile side up, on a flat surface.

Most commercial rug cleaners will clean hooked rugs. Self-service dry-cleaning machines can also be used. Do not, however, put a hooked rug in a washing machine or in any other machine that uses suction to extract the water from the fabric in the rinse cycle. This can loosen the pile on the rug. For rugs hooked with wool yarn, washing is not recommended; dry cleaning or dry rug shampoos are suggested instead. Clean a fine wool yarn rug the same way you would an Oriental or any other fine rug.

Repairing a Hooked Rug

Repair your rug as soon as you see any sign of fraying or loss of pile. Just a few loose loops spread very quickly. There are three kinds of problems—fraying, excess straining, and raveling.

Fraying is caused by excess wear. Fraying of the loops or pile usually means that a bump, or high spot, on the underside of the rug is causing the same area on the reverse, or right side, to take more than its share of wear. Or, the fraying could come from unusually heavy wear on one section of the rug, such as the area in front of a chair.

If your rug is frayed, shake it well; examine the frayed area; check the lining, hemming, backing, and seaming to be sure that a lump or raised area is not causing the fraying. If there is a lump, try to mend the back to make it smooth. If the frayed areas involve the backing as well as the pile, it is best to mend by rehooking. The original backing does not have to be removed. Cut a patch of new backing that is about 2 inches larger than the frayed area. Place the patch over the back side of the frayed area and lightly hem it to the original backing. Note that this will not work if the backing has been latexed. The latex or rubberizing will prevent the double hooking necessary for mending.

Remove the hooked loops and pile, or, if they are really weak, you can rehook right over the worn pile. If you do remove the pile, do so very gently, cutting away when necessary, and pulling the pile from the backing gently, a few strands at a time. The less pull and tug, the better. There should now be a bald area in your rug and a double backing. Rehook through the double backing to replace the open area. Try to blend your new work into any existing design or color. New yarn, even of the same color and dye batch, will look different from the worn material, but it should wear together before long.

If latex or a rubberized backing is used, the solution is more difficult. In this case, you will have to cut away the worn section of the rug. This will leave an ugly hole or tattered end. Using a backing similar to the original backing, cover the area to fill the hole or complete the rug edge. Pin, tape, or use rubber cement to secure the edges of the new fabric to the old. When the new fabric backing is secure, use a sharp curved needle, such as an upholstery needle, to hem the new backing in position. Then rehook the blank area. The blending of new and old is sometimes difficult in this sort of patching, and often the rugs must be washed or even dyed to make them seem all of a piece. When the bald spot has been rehooked, relatex the back of the rug, lightly going over the old work and smoothing the latex to bind the patch and the old backing together. Allow the latex to dry well.

Repairing worn edges is easier than repairing holes. If a border or edge is terribly worn, you might want to unravel the border, and just turn under the backing that held the removed pile. It is also possible to remove the worn border and hem a new wide band of backing material around the edges of the rug.

The rug patterns do not have to be symmetrical. If one section of a border is worn you can use that worn section for rehooking a new motif, or extending the rug at that edge. A floral pattern might acquire a gold frame, or the name of a small animal might be written in script beneath its picture.

Round and oval rugs are more of a challenge. But, as in all hooked rugs, anything goes. A fringe, homemade or commercially made, can be added to the edge of a round or oval rug to protect the edge, disguise a worn area, or make the rug appear larger. If you wish to repair a round or oval rug by rehooking, use the same process as described for a straight-edge rug, but, to form the new backing, overlap a series of small strips of backing fabric one with the other. A round rug will require many such pieces, an oval fewer.

You can also use a single piece of backing for the same purpose, if you prefer. Place the rug on a piece of new backing and, being sure to allow adequate backing for a flat, firm hem, follow the rug size as a guide to cutting the new edge. This method will take more backing material than the strip method, but the effect will be neater.

Storing Your Rug

No matter how much you love your rug, there will be times—perhaps in the midsummer—when you'd like to store it someplace safe. If so, shake the rug free of all loose dirt and foreign matter before storing. It is best to air the rug a few hours outdoors before packing it away.

When packing, try not to fold the rug. Roll it instead, backing side in, pile side out. Rolling it with pile out places less stress on the pile by not squeezing it together. Generally, rugs are easy to store. A nice, tightly rolled rug can be stored in the back of a closet. If the rug is wool, be sure that it is clean and free of stains and grease spots before storing. If you are temporarily storing a rug, you can drape it over a curtain rod or dowel rod hung against the back of a closet. Do not use clothespins, pins, or any kind of fastening, as the weight of the rug against those pins will tear the backing.

Treating a rug with moth preventative, rolling it carefully pile side out, and storing it inside a plastic bag, will keep a rug in excellent condition indefinitely.

DYES AND DYEING YOUR OWN MATERIAL

Yarn, rags, and strips of all kinds are often used in hooking. Dyeing your own yarn, or dyeing old and multicolored woven strips, can give your rug a special old-time and personal look. By experimenting with different colors and different shades, you can sometimes come up with pretty, but unexpected, hues and have a lot of fun in the process.

Dyeing Old and Faded Materials or Rugs

If you want to dye some old and faded rugs, there are some simple rules to follow:

—All the material must be cleaned first. If using an old rug, be sure that it is clean and free of dust and dirt. Remove as much of the old dye as possible by bleaching or washing in baking-soda solution.

—Wash the rug in soapsuds, and rinse thoroughly in warm water. The wool should be clean and thoroughly wet before it is placed in the dyebath.

—Place the wool in the dyebath, being certain that is is completely covered by the liquid.

—After removing the wool from the dyebath, rinse it thoroughly in lukewarm water until the rinse water runs clear.

—Some dyers prefer that the dyebath be heated to the simmering point before the wool is placed in the liquid. In any case, NEVER boil the dyebath during the dyeing process.

—Alum is used as a mordant for most vegetable dyes. A mordant is a caustic substance that fixes or sets colors in dyeing. All the materials should be wet before entering the mordant and should be well covered by the mordant when immersed.

—Some of the chemicals that are used for mordanting are poisonous if swallowed. They should be kept away from children and used for no purpose other than fabric dyeing.

—Remember, it is impossible to dye an originally dark color and get a light color: dark brown cannot be dyed light yellow. Only light pink, beige, or off-white can successfully be dyed pale yellow, pink, or light green. Light yellow, green, violet, and blue-gray materials can be dyed dark blue or brown.

—Mixtures of yellow and blue dyes can be used to produce shades of green. Likewise, mixtures of red and yellow dyes can be used for orange, bronze, and gold-brown colors. Reds and blues can be used to produce violets and purples.

—Most light colors can easily be dyed and redyed. They will have a new, fresh look that will probably add years to an old rug, or give added sparkle to a new rug made from recycled yarn.

Dye Recipes

Deep Yellow
4 qts. marigold blossoms
1 tsp. alum (mordant)
1 lb. washed wet wool

Cover the flowers with water in a large enameled pot, and cook for about one hour. Strain and return the liquid to the pot. Discard the cooked blossoms. Add enough water to cover the wool. Add alum and stir thoroughly into the dyebath until the alum is completely dissolved. When the dyebath begins to simmer, add the wet wool. Add enough hot water to cover the wool. Simmer for 30 minutes.

Remove the wool and rinse thoroughly in lukewarm water. Squeeze out surplus water and hang the wool to dry. Do not dry on a radiator or in a drier; sunlight and fresh air are preferable.

Orange-Gold
4 qts. marigold blossoms
½ tsp. tin (stannous chloride)
½ tsp. cream of tartar
1 lb. washed wet wool

Follow same procedure for deep yellow dye. Instead of mordanting in alum, use tin and cream of tartar.

Yellow Shades
1 lb. onion skins (outer skins of *yellow* onions)
1½ oz. alum
1 lb. washed wet wool

Cover the onion skins with water in a large enameled pot, and cook for about one hour. Strain and return the liquid to the pot. Discard the onion skins. Add enough water to cover the wool. Add alum and stir thoroughly into the dyebath until the alum is completely dissolved. When the dyebath begins to simmer, add the wet wool. Add enough hot water to cover the wool. Simmer for 30 minutes.

Remove the wool and rinse thoroughly in lukewarm water. Squeeze out surplus water and hang the wool to dry. Do not dry on a radiator or in a drier; sunlight is preferable.

Brass Color
1 lb. onion skins (outer skins of *yellow* onions)
½ oz. chrome (potassium bichromate)
1 lb. washed wet wool

Follow same procedure for yellow shades. Instead of mordanting in alum, use chrome.

Greenish-Gold
1 lb. onion skins (outer skins of *red* onions)
½ oz. chrome
1 lb. washed wet wool

Follow same procedure for yellow shades; but use red onion skins, and mordant in chrome.

Fresh dandelion roots can also be used to dye wool. Mordanting with chrome (potassium bichromate) will produce a creamy green tint; mordanting with copper (copper sulphate) will produce a dark green.

When dyeing with natural plants, some dyers prefer to use vinegar or ordinary table salt in place of any other mordant. Do experiment with various mordants on small quantities of wool. As with rug hooking, do not lock yourself into rigid procedures.

A GALLERY OF PATTERNS

Floral: Hooked yarn on burlap 32" x 59". A well-balanced design in red, brown, pink, and blue. Mid-nineteenth century. Courtesy Dalmar Tift and Ilon Spect. The pattern for the corner section and center piece are given at ⅓ of the actual size.

BORDER PATTERN 1

2

BORDER PATTERN 2

PATTERN 2

Pictorial: Hooked rag on burlap, 22.5" x 36". A brown and white dog on tan ground with floral pattern for border in pink and green. Twentieth century. Courtesy Dalmar Tift and Ilon Spect.
The pattern for corner and center piece are given at ¼ of the actual size.

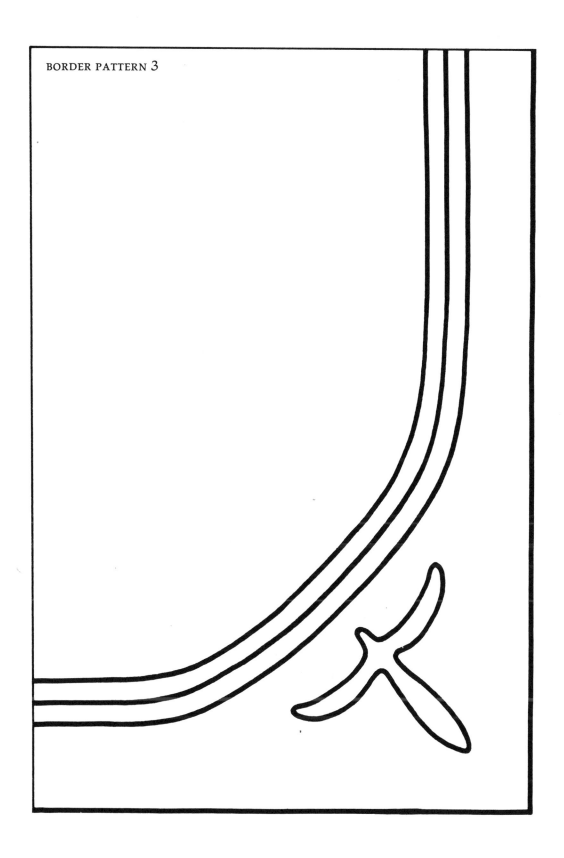

3

BORDER PATTERN 3

PATTERN **3**

Pictorial: Hooked yarn on burlap, 31" x 45".
Houses in red and yellow with a red boat on the blue lake, green trees and brown fields. Twentieth century. Courtesy Dalmar Tift and Ilon Spect.
The pattern for corner and center piece are given at ¼ of the actual size.

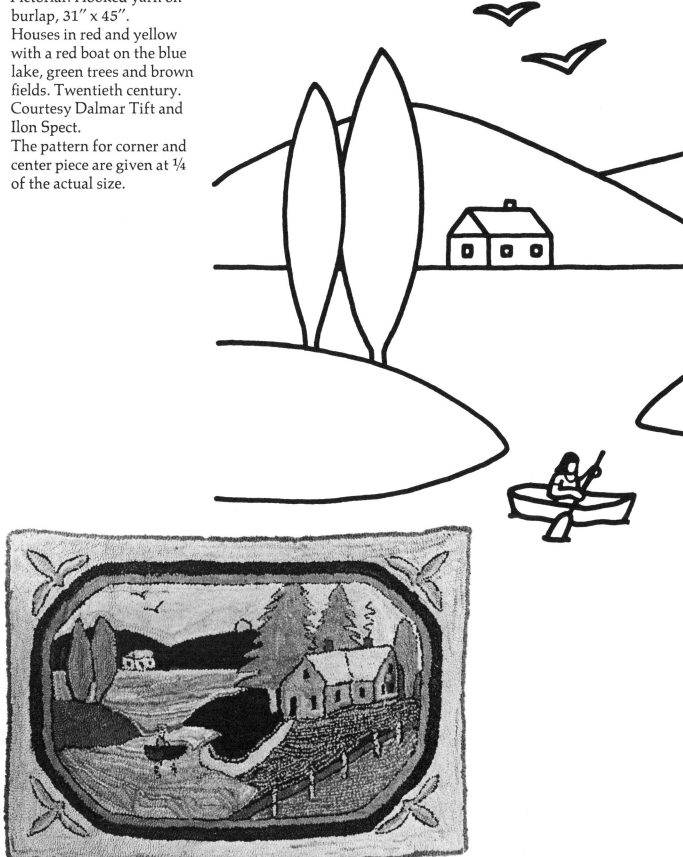

4

PATTERN 4

Pictorial: Hooked rag on burlap,
38″ x 14″. A tan dog on black
ground with red and white floral
border. Late nineteenth century.
Courtesy Dalmar Tift and Ilon
Spect.
The pattern for the corner and
center piece are given at ¼ of the
actual size.

BORDER PATTERN 4

5

BORDER PATTERN 5

Pictorial: Hooked rag on burlap, 19" x 30". White geese on gray ground with green trees and yellow sun. Late nineteenth century. Courtesy Dalmar Tift and Ilon Spect. The pattern for the corner is given at ¼ of the actual size. The detail is ½ of the actual size.

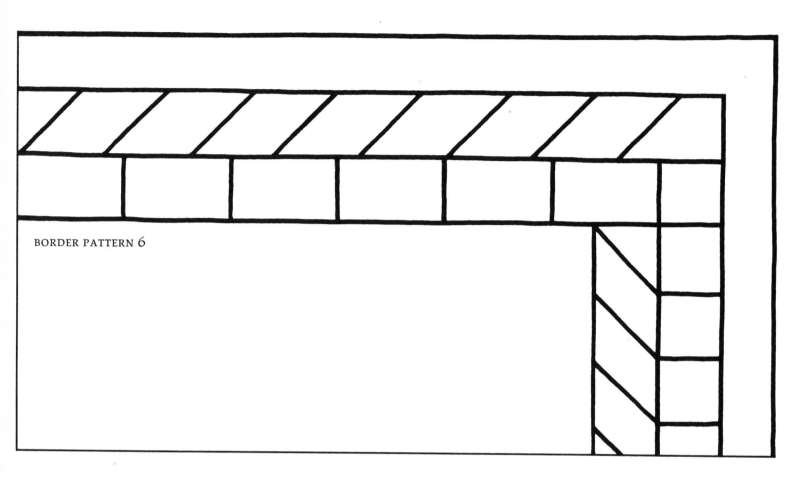

6

BORDER PATTERN 6

Geometric: Clipped, hooked yarn on burlap, 25" x 46". Design reminiscent of Southwest American Indian art. Predominant colors are wine, tan, aquamarine, and umber. Remains of tassel border. Late nineteenth century. Courtesy Dalmar Tift and Ilon Spect.

The pattern for the corner is given at ¼ of the actual size. The detail is ½ of the actual size.

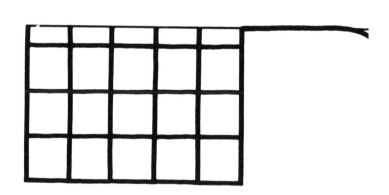

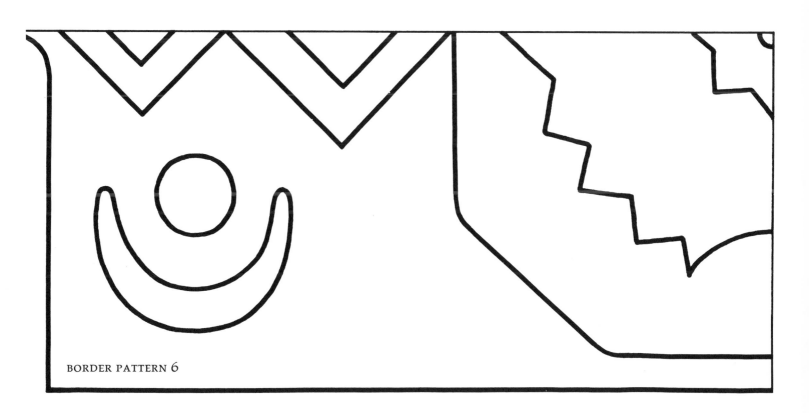

BORDER PATTERN 6

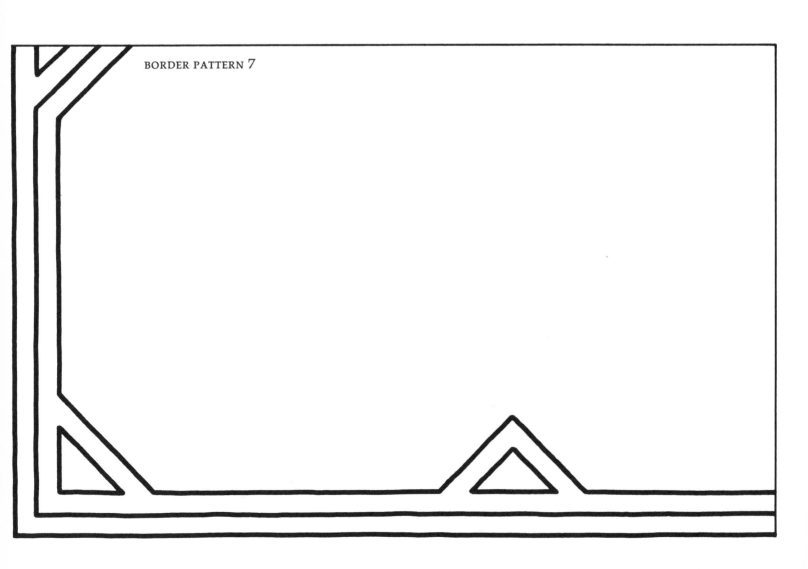

7

BORDER PATTERN 7

PATTERN 7

Pictorial: Hooked rag on burlap, 24" x 39.5". Spectacular red and green peacock against a pink sky and green grass. Late nineteenth century. Courtesy Dalmar Tift and Ilon Spect.

The pattern for the corner is given at ¼ of the actual size. The detail is ½ of the actual size.

BORDER PATTERN 8

PATTERN 8

Floral-geometric: Hooked yarn on burlap, 36.5" x 54". Red berries and green leaves on a tan ground surrounded by tile in wine, red, green, blue, and yellow. Twentieth century. Courtesy Dalmar Tift and Ilon Spect.
The pattern for the corner is given at ¼ of the actual size. The detail is also ¼ of the actual size.

BORDER PATTERN 9

Pictorial-geometric: Hooked rag on burlap, 22" x 50". Horseshoes and stars in a basically geometric composition featuring green, pink, blue, white, brown, and umber. An unusual type from the late nineteenth century. Courtesy Dalmar Tift and Ilon Spect.

The pattern for the corner is given at ¼ of the actual size. The detail is ½ of the actual size.

PATTERN 10

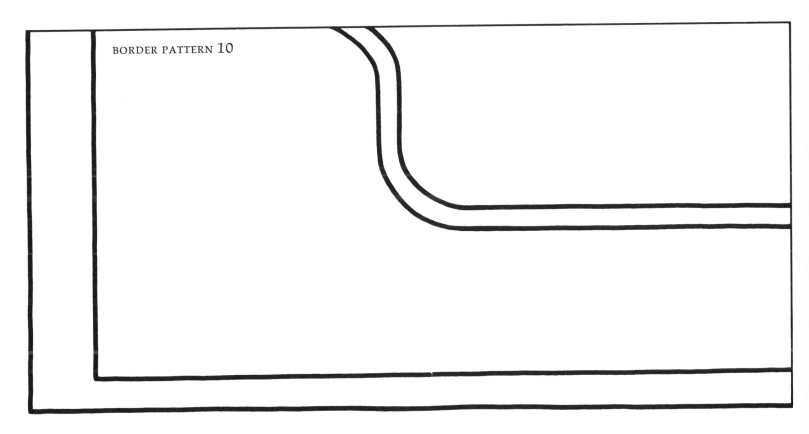

BORDER PATTERN 10

Pictorial: Hooked yarn on burlap, 18″
x 38.5″. Brown and white cat on a red
pillow with red and brown floral
border. Late nineteenth century. Courtesy Dalmar Tift and Ilon Spect.
The pattern for the center and corner
piece is given at ¼ of the actual size.
The detail is given full size.

PATTERN 10

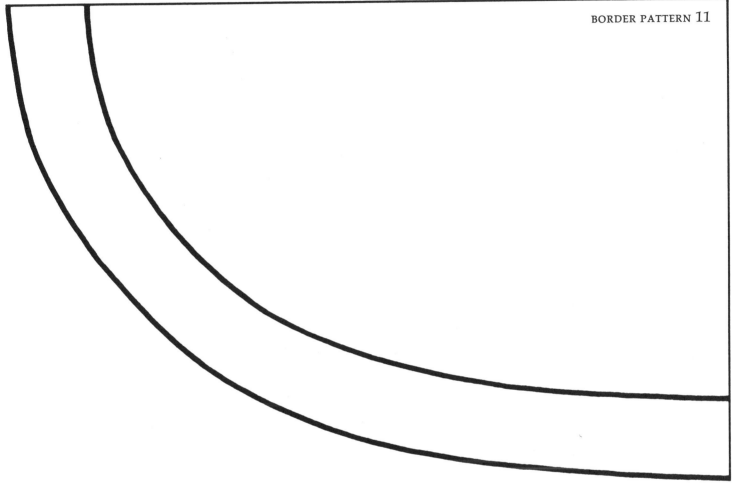

Floral: Hooked yarn and rag on burlap, 34" x 52.5". Leaves and flowers in green, purple, and white on a tan background. Late nineteenth century. Courtesy Dalmar Tift and Ilon Spect.

The pattern for the corner is ¼ of the actual size. The detail is given full size.

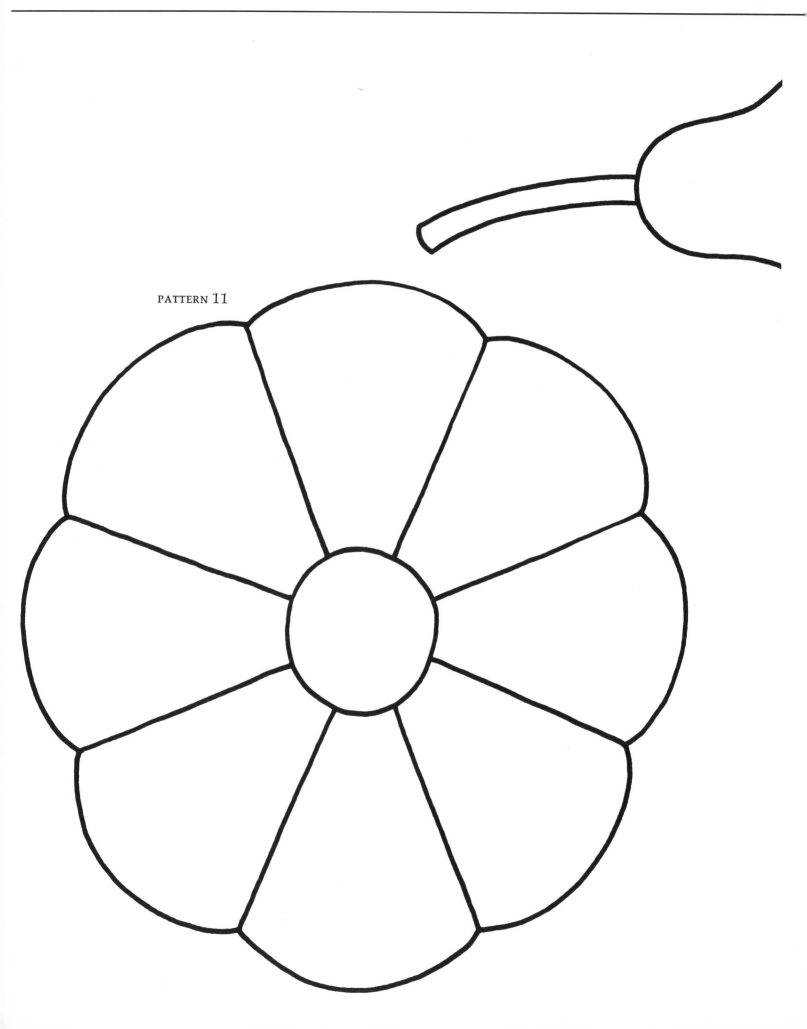

PATTERN 11

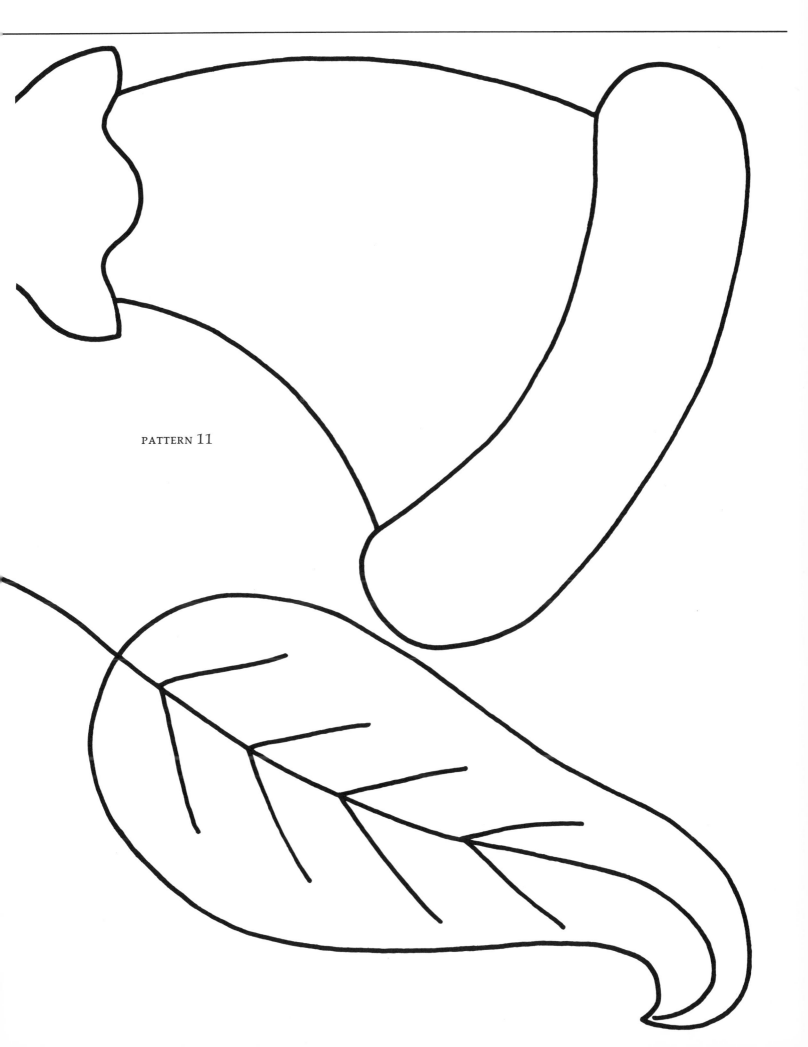

PATTERN 11

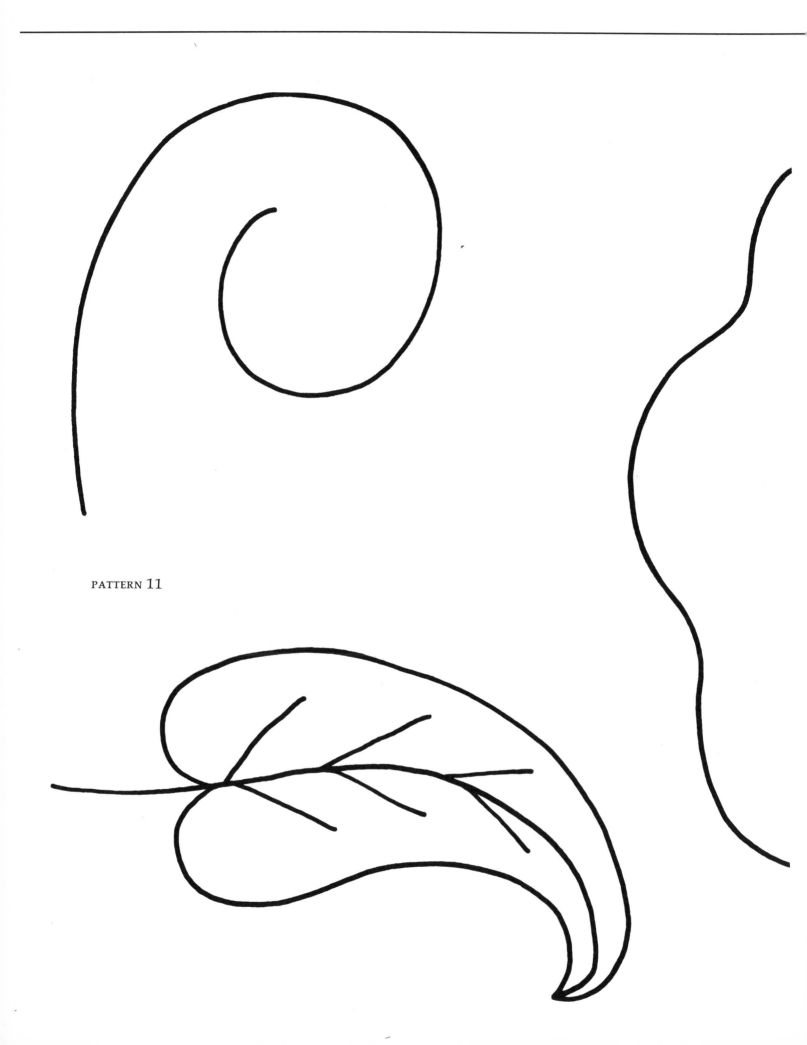

PATTERN 11

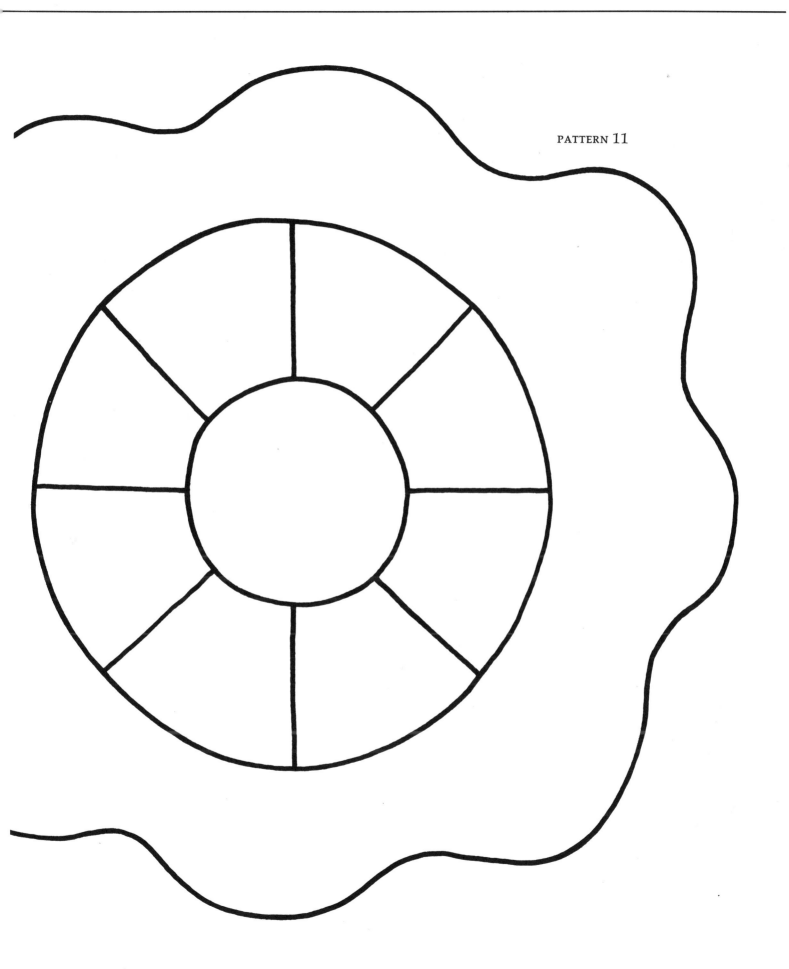

PATTERN 11

BORDER PATTERN 12

Floral: Clipped, hooked rag on burlap, 38.5" x 69". Elaborate Jardiniere rug in shades of green, tan, and brown. Mid-nineteenth century. Courtesy Dalmar Tift and Ilon Spect.
The pattern for the corner and the center piece are both ⅓ of the actual size.

PATTERN 12

13

BORDER PATTERN 13

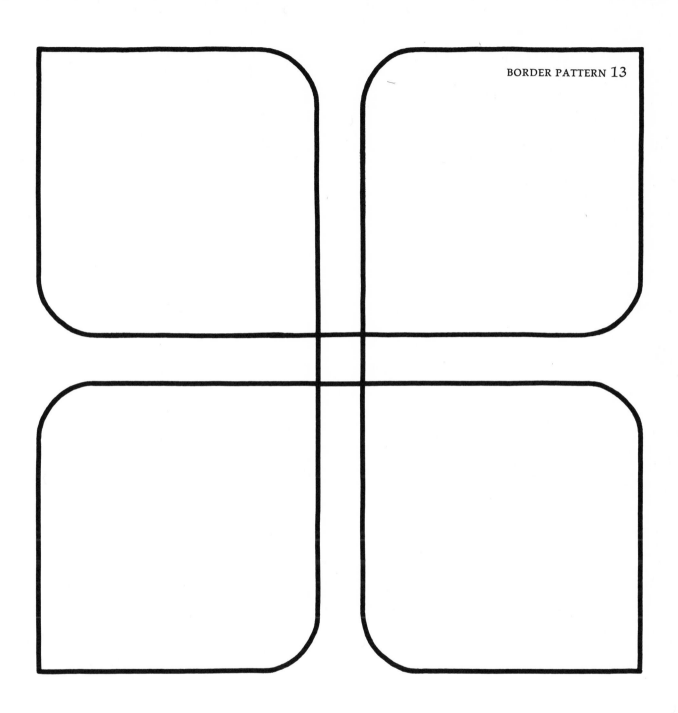

BORDER PATTERN 13

Geometric: Hooked rag on burlap, 28.5″ x 39.5″. Pale green and tan devices surrounded by a purple border. Twentieth century. Dalmar Tift and Ilon Spect.
The pattern for the corner is ⅓ of the actual size. The detail is shown full size.

14

PATTERN 14

Floral: Hooked rag on burlap, 30″ x 31.5″. An extremely primitive and abstract floral in shades of blue, brown, yellow, rust, and green. Mid-nineteenth century. Courtesy Dalmar Tift and Ilon Spect.
The pattern for the corner is ¼ of the actual size.
The detail is given full size.

BORDER PATTERN 14

PATTERN 15

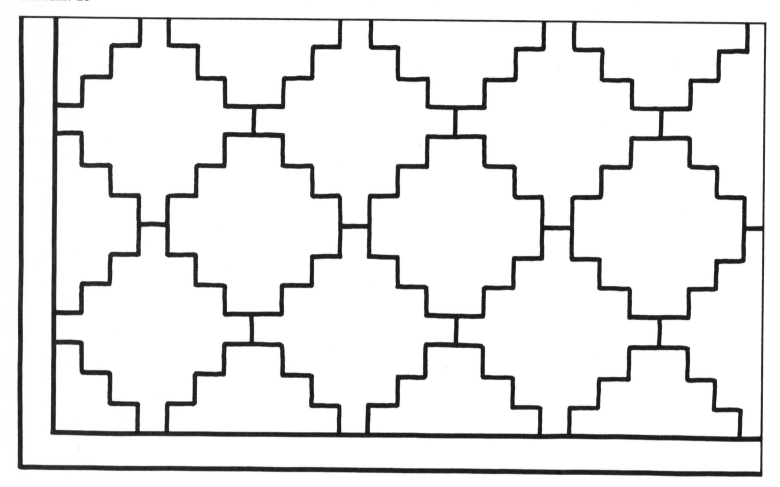

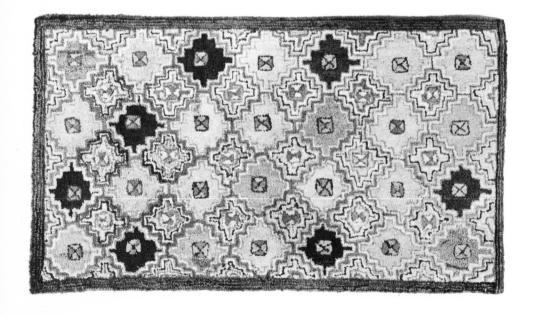

Geometric: Hooked rag on burlap, 29" x 51.5". Cross pattern in red, blue, yellow, orange, and tan, with gray "hit or miss" border. Late nineteenth century. Courtesy Dalmar Tift and Ilon Spect.

The pattern for the corner is ¼ of the actual size.

16

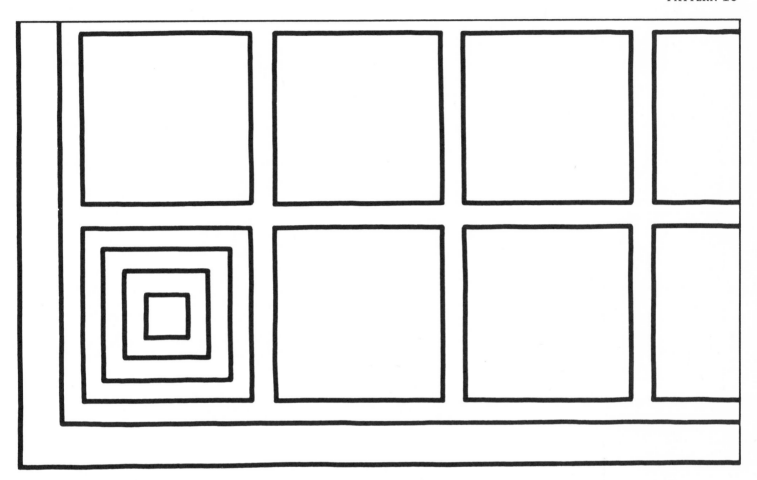

Geometric: Hooked yarn on burlap, 27" x 46". Squares in blue, gray, wine, black, and yellow surrounded by gray "hit or miss" border. Twentieth century. Courtesy Dalmar Tift and Ilon Spect.
The pattern for the corner is ¼ of the actual size.

PATTERN 17

Floral-Geometric: hooked yarn and burlap on burlap, 22.5" x 39.5". Red and green flowers on a white field surrounded by square and column pattern in black, red, green, blue, and tan. Late nineteenth century. Courtesy Dalmar Tift and Ilon Spect.

The pattern for the corner is ¼ of the actual size. The detail is given at ½ of the actual size.

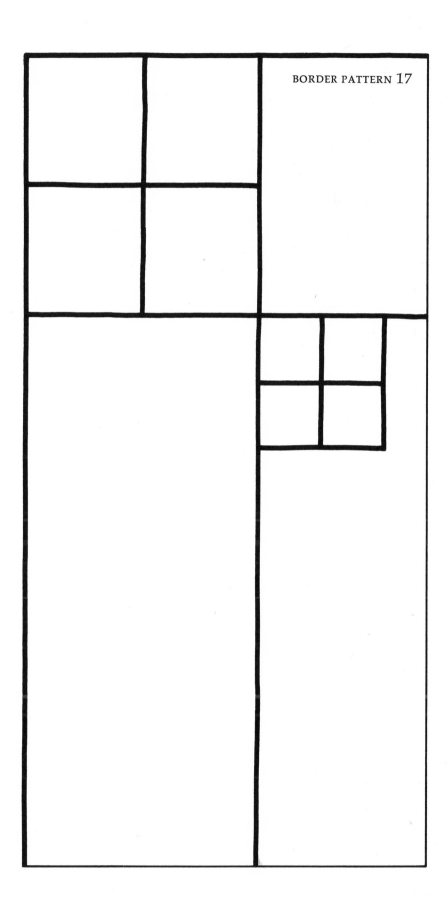

BORDER PATTERN 17

18

Geometric: Hooked yarn and rag on burlap, 22" x 34". Squares in red, black, salmon, gray, orange, and blue, with a tan and purple border. Twentieth century Courtesy Dalmar Tift and Ilon Spect.
The pattern for the corner is ¼ of the actual size.

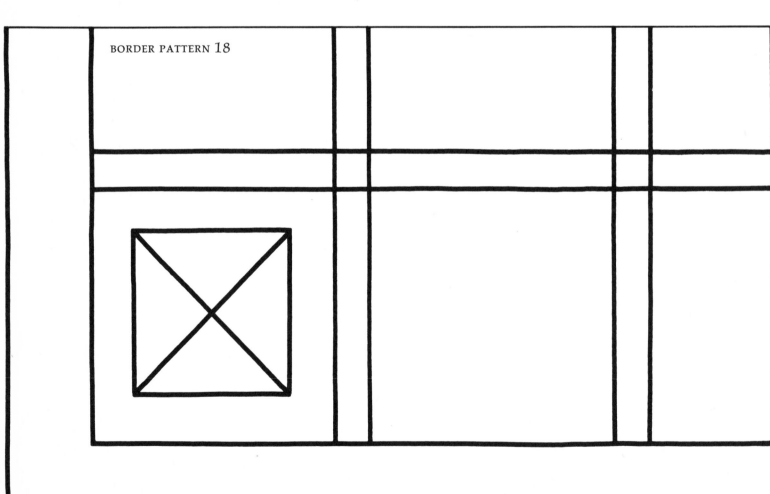

BORDER PATTERN 18

Floral-Geometric: Hooked rag on burlap, 32.5" x 36.5". Flowers in rose and green on a black and tan ground. Twentieth century. Courtesy Dalmar Tift and Ilon Spect. The pattern for the corner is ¼ of the actual size. The detail is shown at ½ of the actual size.

PATTERN 19

BORDER PATTERN 19

20

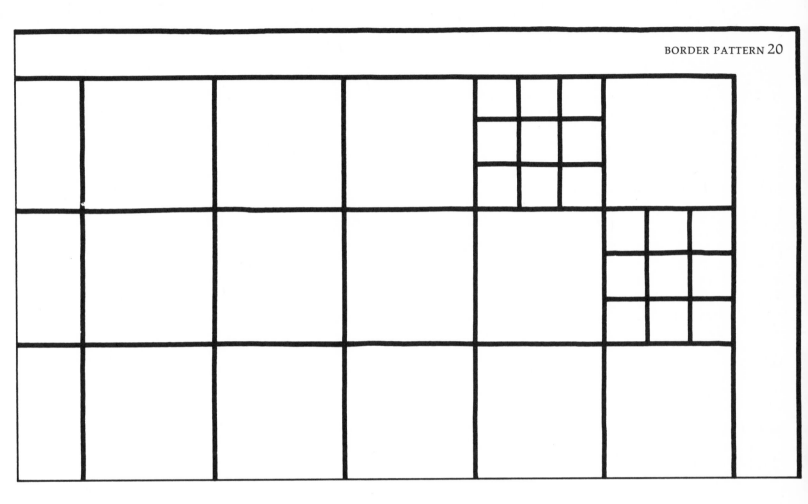

Geometric: Hooked yarn on burlap, 28″ x 51″. Crosses and columns in purple, red, blue, wine, gray, and white with a black border. Twentieth century. Courtesy Dalmar Tift and Ilon Spect. The pattern for the cover is ¼ of the actual size.

PATTERN 21

Pictorial: Hooked yarn on burlap, 16" x 22.5". A white swan with yellow beak floats on a blue pond surrounded by green rushes beneath a gray sky. Gray "hit or miss" border. Late nineteenth century. Courtesy Dalmar Tift and Ilon Spect.

The pattern for the corner is ¼ of the actual size.

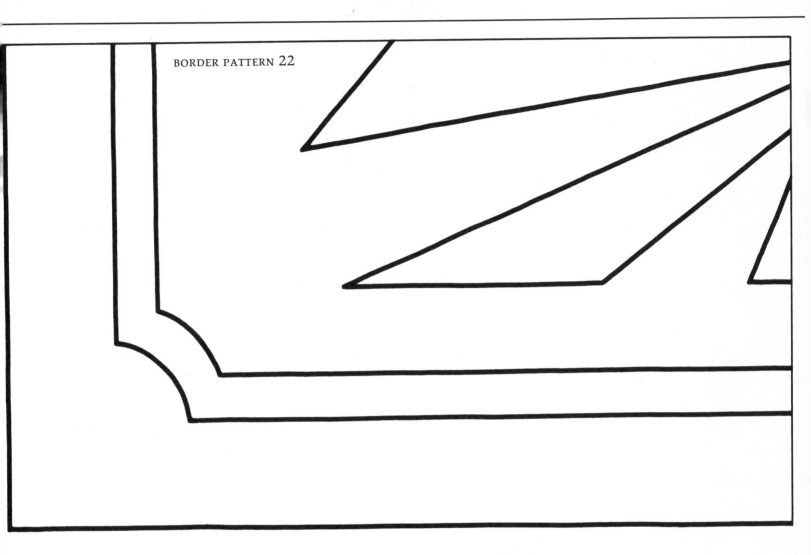

BORDER PATTERN 22

Geometric: Hooked yarn and rag on burlap,
24″ x 40″. Stylized sunburst in pink, orange,
and red against a gray ground; bordered in
black. Late nineteenth century. Courtesy
Dalmar Tift and Ilon Spect.
The pattern for the corner is ¼ of the actual size.

Floral: Hooked rag on burlap, 32" x 58". Rolling floral border in rose, red, and black, with blank gray central area. Typical of patterns which provided open space into which rug hooker might work her own or other patterns. Late nineteenth century. Courtesy Dalmar Tift and Ilon Spect.

The pattern for the corner is ¼ of the actual size.

PATTERN 23

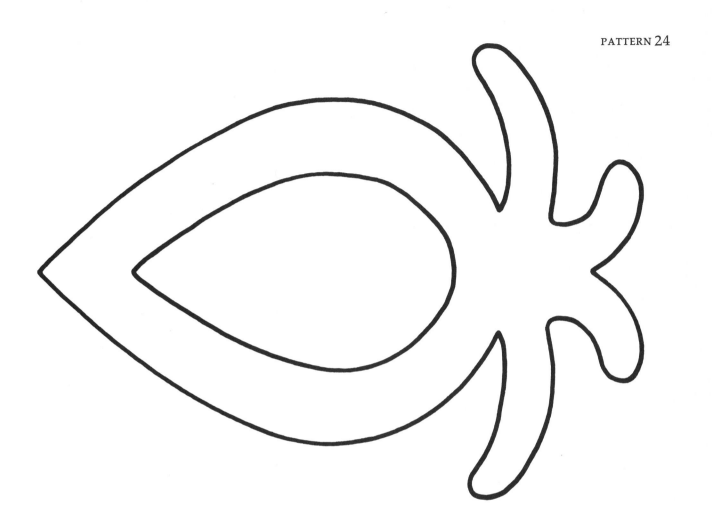

Floral: Hooked yarn and rag on burlap, 18.5″ x 32″. A pleasing pattern in shades of red, green, blue, and gray. Mid-nineteenth century. Courtesy Dalmar Tift and Ilon Spect.
The pattern for the corner is ¼ of the actual size. The center is ½ of the actual size. The corner detail is full size.

PATTERN 24

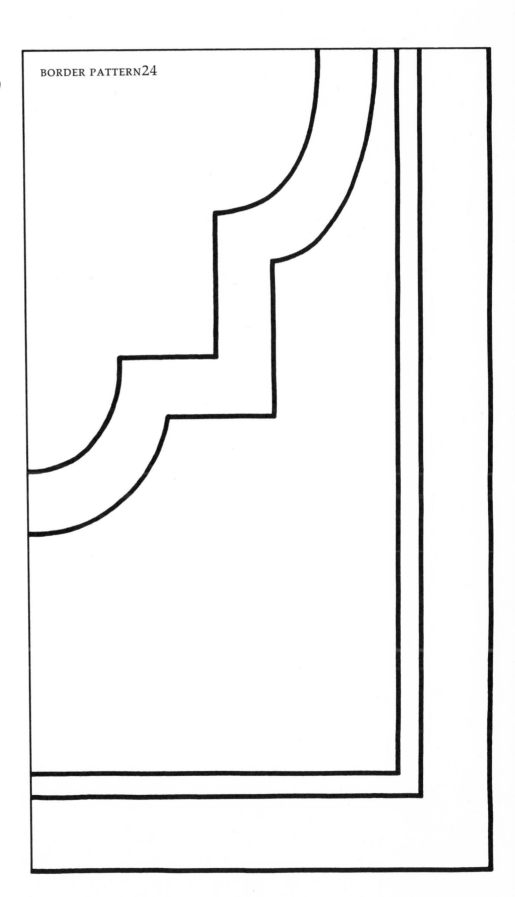

BORDER PATTERN 24

A GALLERY OF PATTERNS

Pictorial: Hooked rag on burlap, 18" x 34.5". Entrance or door mat featuring a white house against a gray ground with unusual gray and black border. Mid-nineteenth century. Courtesy Dalmar Tift and Ilon Spect.

The pattern for the corner is ¼ of the actual size. The house is shown ½ size; the flowers are full size.

PATTERN 25

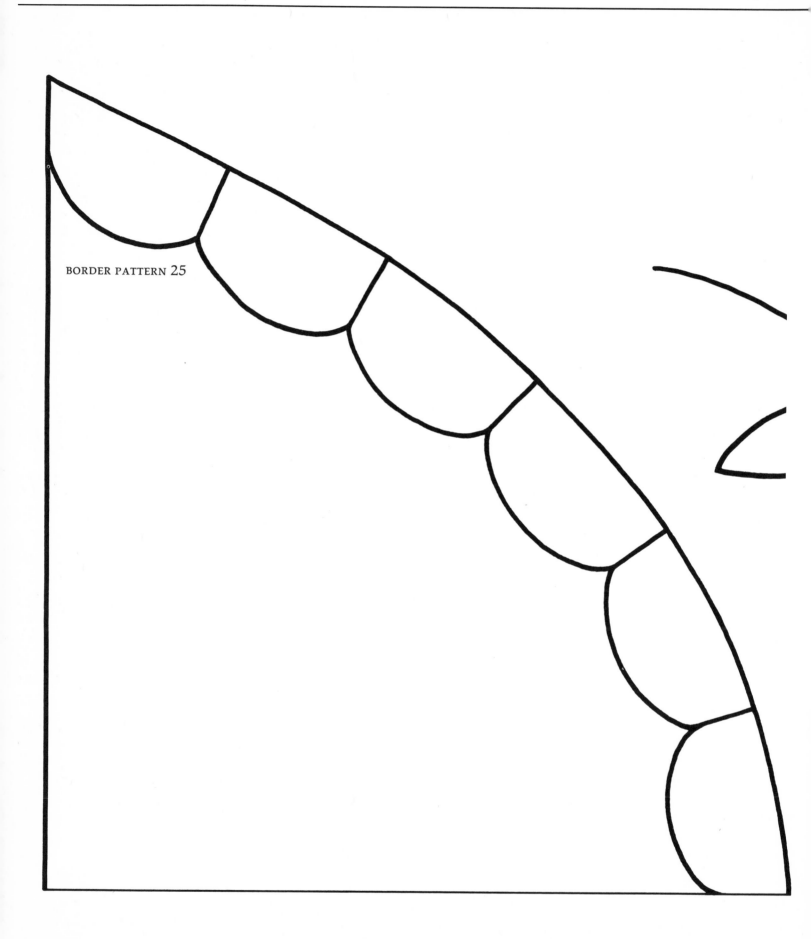

BORDER PATTERN 25

PATTERN 25

PATTERN 25

SUPPLIERS OF HOOKED-RUG EQUIPMENT

Lincoln House
Old Sturbridge Village
Sturbridge, Massachusetts 01566

Norden Crafts
222 Waukegan Road
Glenview, Illinois

The Ruggery
565 Cedar Swamp Road
Glen Head, L.I., New York 11545

Columbia-Minerva
295 Fifth Avenue
New York, New York 10016

The Handcraft Shoppe
25 Old Kings Highway North
Darien, Connecticut 06820

Rittermere Crafts Studio
P.O. Box 240
Vineland, Ontario,
Canada

Laure's
City Line Craft Shop
252-03 Northern Boulevard
Little Neck, New York 11363

Coulter Studios, Inc.
138 East 60th Street
New York, New York 10023

Flo Ann Gordon *Mordants:*
P.O. Box 506
Roseburg, Oregon 97470

Hook and Needle
1869 E. State Street
Westport, Connecticut

Edith Dana
Edana Designs
196 W. Norwood Road
Darien, Connecticut 06820

Ruth J. Davis
Yankee Peddler Designs
49 Pleasant Avenue
Trumbull, Connecticut 06611

Happy Di Franza
Di Franza Designs
25 Bow Street
North Reading, Massachusetts

Harry M. Fraser
192 Hartford Road
Manchester, Connecticut 06040

Heirloom Rugs
28 Harlem Street
Rumford, Rhode Island 02916

Pam Jones
New Earth Designs
Appleton Park
Ipswich, Massachusetts 01938

Geneva Lapham
Karlkraft-Cheva Designs
Severs Bridge Road
South Merrimac, New Hampshire 03083

Whitney Patterns
Main Street
Harwichport, Massachusetts 02646

The Elements
14 R Lewis Street
Greenwich, Connecticut 06830

BIBLIOGRAPHY

Boyles, Margaret, *Rugmaking*, Vol. 785, Columbia-Minerva Corp., New York, 1975.

Depas, Spencer, *Textile Art: Macramé, Weaving, and Tapestry*, Macmillan, New York, 1973.

Dillmont, Th.de, *Encyclopedia of Needlework*, DMC publications, France, 1971.

Dye Plants and Dyeing—A Handbook, Brooklyn Botanic Garden Record, Vol. 20, No. 3, Brooklyn, New York 11225, 1964.

Eichelberger, Catherine U., *Hooked Rugs*, Cornell University Misc. Bulletin #43, New York State College of Home Economics, Ithaca, New York, 1968.

Grae, Ida, *Nature's Colors*, Macmillan, New York, 1974.

Johnson, P., Moseley, S., Koenig, H., *Crafts Design, Illustrated Guide*, Wadsworth Publishing Company, Belmont, California, 1962.

Kopp, Joel and Kate, *American Hooked and Sewn Rugs, Folk Art Underfoot*, E. P. Dutton, New York, 1975.

Krochmal, Arnold and Connie, *The Complete Illustrated Book of Dyes from Natural Sources*, Doubleday & Company, Garden City, New York, 1974.

Moshimer, Joan, *The Complete Rug Hooker*, New York Graphic Society, New York, 1975.

Znamierowski, Nell, *Step-by-Step Rugmaking*, Golden Press, New York, 1969.

INDEX